LEARNING TO PRAY

ALSO BY WAYNE MULLER

Sabbath
How, Then, Shall We Live?
Legacy of the Heart

LEARNING

TO

PRAY

How We Find

Heaven on Earth

Wayne Muller

B a n t a m   B o o k s

New York   Toronto   London   Sydney   Auckland

LEARNING TO PRAY
A Bantam Book / May 2003

Published by
Bantam Dell
A Division of Random House, Inc.
New York, New York

All rights reserved.
Copyright © 2003 by Wayne Muller

BOOK DESIGN BY GLEN EDELSTEIN

No part of this book may be reproduced or transmitted in any form or by any means, electronic or mechanical, including photocopying, recording, or by any information storage and retrieval system, without the written permission of the publisher, except where permitted by law.

Bantam Books is a registered trademark of Random House, Inc., and the colophon is a trademark of Random House, Inc.

Library of Congress Cataloging in Publication Data
Muller, Wayne.
Learning to pray : how we find heaven on earth / by Wayne Muller.
p.   cm.
ISBN 0-553-10553-1
1. Lord's Prayer.   2. Prayer—Christianity.
BV215 .M79 2003   2003041841

Manufactured in the United States of America
Published simultaneously in Canada

10 9 8 7 6 5 4 3 2 1
RRH

For my Mother,
who taught me to pray

and

For Loretta Barrett,
who first believed
in this book

LEARNING TO PRAY

PRELUDE

In northern California, there is fog in the morning.

As I write this, looking out my window, I know that the mountains and the trees, the grasses and the sky, remain hidden in the fog, but I cannot see them with my eyes. Instead, I feel their presence in my body, I know the shapes that lie behind the fog for having seen them, watched them emerge again and again. It is a primitive kind of faith, based on repetition and proof, but a kind of faith that the fog will, indeed, lift. Slowly, as the sun warms the earth, the fog begins to clear. And as it does, outlines appear, colors, textures, and, finally, the sky and sun are quietly revealed and I can see them all.

This is prayer. This is deep, faithful listening, waiting for what is hidden to be revealed. Prayer is not words;

prayer is what happens when you listen and wait, beneath the words, for the outline of heaven to emerge.

Every day there are moments when I find myself drawn to pray. I pray because I must, because regardless of my good intentions I lose my bearings. I make mistakes. I am stopped by the way the world challenges and confounds my plans. When a loved one is beset by illness, ache, or fear, I pray their healing may be deep and true. When I feel suddenly lost or lonely, I pray for the comfort of a nourishing spirit that will teach me, show me the way. At other times my prayer is filled with gratefulness for the numberless blessings showered on my life. In these moments, my prayer is astonishingly simple: *Thank you.*

One of the prayers I turn to again and again is the Lord's Prayer. I pray it daily, alone in my room in front of my altar, and on long walks in the hills behind my home. I have prayed it in countless churches, in twelve-step meetings with alcoholics and drug addicts, and in the intimate company of friends and loved ones.

I have prayed it with Christians, Buddhists, Hindus, and Native Americans, Muslims, and agnostics. Beneath the cadence of these familiar words we are united in our deep and universal yearning for connection with the Divine. I have used it as a meditation at countless gatherings with teachers, physicians, counselors, social workers, parents, nurses, community activists, clergy, and chaplains as we explore how our inner spiritual pilgrimage clearly shapes our capacity to do our good and necessary work in the world.

I offer this book as a guide for those who are unsure about how to pray. Perhaps we feel awkward or uncomfortable, not knowing the "right" way to pray. What should prayer feel like, and what is it supposed to accomplish? Should we pray to get everything we want, or should we pray instead to accept what we have been given? Or does prayer offer something deeper, beyond measurable purpose or effect, serving instead as a precious invitation to simply rest deeply in the gentle, loving company of the Divine?

In the Gospel stories about the men and women who followed Jesus, we hear a poignant echo of our own dilemma. The disciples tried to live spiritual lives, to become healers and teachers like Jesus. But whenever things went wrong, they lost their confidence. When confronted with a hungry crowd, they became anxious and worried about how they would feed everyone. When their boat was being tossed by a storm, they trembled and became afraid. When people bombarded them with requests for healing, they despaired over how it would all get done.

In the midst of their own confusion, they saw in Jesus something they hoped to find in themselves. He remained strong and wise, even in the most trying moments. The sick and wounded pursued him, clamoring for his time, his healing touch, his words. Yet even as people crowded around him, Jesus drew upon some reservoir of seemingly endless kindness. He had infinite patience for anyone in need.

For years they followed him, watching him, listening to him, trying to be like him, to learn his ways, to do what he did. They devoted their lives to becoming as wise as Jesus. But despite their most persistent efforts, they often found themselves discouraged and disappointed.

Jesus knew something that the disciples were not yet able to understand. Jesus knew how to live on the earth while trusting the wisdom of the Spirit. Leaving behind the pressing call to serve others, he would regularly retreat to a quiet place, where he would remain still and listen for the clear inner voice that would refresh him and remind him what was beautiful, necessary, and true.

Jesus knew how to pray. Just as there is a time for every purpose under heaven, there is a time to serve, and a time to pray. Jesus respected this delicate rhythm. So in the morning, Jesus would leave everyone behind, go off to a solitary place, and anchor his life in deep, nourishing prayer.

Even in their disquietude, his disciples saw how he was changed when he returned from prayer. They felt something different in the way he touched, the way he spoke, the way he listened, and waited, and remained at peace. When they saw him with the poor, with the hungry, with the lame and the lepers, he was so calm, so kind, so unafraid. They wanted to feel what Jesus felt. They wanted to be that clear, that whole. They wanted to feel his peace and wisdom in their own hearts and minds. It was painful to lose their way, to be so quickly lost and frightened, to live without some taste of heaven on earth.

Finally, they came to Jesus and asked him:

Teach us to pray.

And so it was that Jesus taught them these words:

Our Father,

who art in heaven,

Hallowed be thy name.

Thy kingdom come,

thy will be done,

on earth, as it is in heaven.

Give us this day our daily bread.

And forgive us our trespasses,

as we forgive those who trespass against us.

And lead us not into temptation,

but deliver us from evil.

For thine is the kingdom,

the power, and the glory,

forever and ever.

Amen.

At this point it is crucial to note that his followers did *not* say, *Give us a prayer.* They clearly asked, *Teach us to*

pray. So when Jesus offers these words, we have to assume he is offering much more than a simple prayer, a unique succession of phrases to be mindlessly repeated in church or hastily recited before bed. The prayer itself is a guide, a teaching story, a finely crafted sequence of instructions on how to pray.

If we listen carefully, every word, every phrase reveals some potent teaching about prayer. The ever-present gift of the prayer lies deeper than the lines we know so well. The words are not the prayer; they are precise doorways into a lifetime of practice.

Within these few words, we can discover all we will ever need to learn about how to pray. Every line is an astonishing gift of wisdom, a subtle teaching that is hidden, as in a Chinese puzzle-box, gently and gradually uncovered and understood through a lifetime of prayerfulness.

My hope is that this book will help you learn to pray. I offer it as a companion, something to hold in your hand and in your heart. Allow each word, each phrase to work on you, to take you more deeply inward. If you are patient and awake, you may find that your eyes, ears, and heart are gently opened, and you may begin to feel what Jesus felt: the gradual, palpable unfolding of heaven on earth.

OUR

When we pray, we never pray alone.

Nowhere in the Lord's Prayer do we find the word *I*. Prayer is not a solitary practice; as prayer guides us inward, we are led into deep communion with everyone who has ever prayed. Beginning with the word *Our,* we cultivate a deep intention to pray on behalf of, and in the company of, the entire family of creation.

We belong to something larger than ourselves. Even in complete solitude, we remain part of a living community. When we pray—when we retreat to a still place of deep listening—even in our intimate seclusion, our prayers reverberate through the connective fabric of life.

When we pray, even as we lift up our own deep needs and yearnings, we also pray for grace, joy, and the alleviation of suffering for all beings. Prayer honors deep, unseen connections that place us in kinship with all beings. Throughout this prayer, we hear the echo of our collective yearning—*our* Father, *our* bread, *our* trespasses.

Sadly, our society seeks to deny the astonishing power of our deep interconnectedness by promoting a corrosive illusion of isolation and self-sufficiency. As we seemingly become more and more self-sufficient in our cars and on our computers, we are trapped by an insidious lie that we can somehow live apart from the subtle dance of interdependence. This is a terrible misunderstanding that does violence to the spirit, and promotes a feeling of being crushed by the weight of deep loneliness.

In truth, countless others accompany us each step of the way, and we do nothing without their assistance. Have we ever grown all our own food, built our own homes, woven the cloth for our own clothing? Every moment we live, we depend on the labor of countless farmers, teachers, doctors, carpenters, truck drivers, nurses, miners, parents, children, artists, loggers, steel workers, cattle, bees, worms, trees—numberless people and beings. When we proudly proclaim that we are "self-sufficient," we deny the nourishment and companionship offered us by the rich family to which we belong.

So when we pray for inner peace and healing, we also seek some benefit for all who are in need. But how can we pray for so many when our own needs seem so immediate? Pulled by too many demands, committed to too many projects, we often feel overwhelmed by the needs of others, and seek in prayer to retreat, to remove ourselves from people, and take refuge in solitude. This is, for many of us, the attraction of prayer.

WHY DO WE PRAY?

I often feel called to pray when I am weary and depleted, when I feel as if the weight of the world were on my shoulders. As much as I resolve to offer my best, to do my work, raise my children, contribute to my community, and be a good friend and useful citizen of the planet, I can feel overwhelmed and discouraged that I have not done more.

But if I look carefully at myself in these moments, I find I have taken on these things as if they were my work alone. Whenever I take on more than I can honorably do, or try to do more than I can honestly handle, something inevitably goes wrong. Then I feel like a failure, disappointed I could not do everything right. In the end, I feel isolated and lonely. It is in times such as these that I find myself needing some solace, seeking comfort and sanctuary in prayer. "In isolation," the Buddha cautions, "lies the world's great misery."

I was newly graduated from Harvard Divinity School when I moved to Santa Fe, New Mexico. There, a group of Plains Indians invited me to take part in a sweat-lodge ceremony. Although I had spent three years studying the world's religions, I had never participated in such a ceremony, and I was more than a little nervous. The temperatures in a sweat lodge can get very high, and I was afraid I wouldn't be able to stand the heat. What if I needed to leave? My hosts were gentle and understanding, and assured me that I could leave when I wished.

They took all day to prepare the fire and arrange the lodge in the manner prescribed by tradition. Willow branches were cut, shaped, and tied to frame the lodge; blankets covered the frame; a fire pit was dug and large rocks were gathered to be placed in the raging fire for several hours. When the time came to begin the ceremony, we all gathered around the lodge. It was winter, it was night, and it was snowing.

The one who tended the fire told me that as I entered the lodge, I must say aloud the words *mitakuye oyasin*—"to all my relations." When Native Americans say "all my relations," they do not mean only grandparents, aunts, uncles, and cousins, although they do include these blood relatives. They also mean to encompass all our relations in the family of creation, the two-legged, the four-legged, the birds and fish and plants and even the trees who gave their lives to make this fire that heats these rocks that make the steam in the sweat lodge.

During this ceremony I learned that "all my relations" was a rich and magnificent acknowledgment of the interconnectedness of all life. We each took turns to speak as we went around the circle, four times in all, offering prayers in each of the four rounds to the four directions, for the earth, for those in need, for the animals on this land, for Father Sky and Mother Earth and all her creatures. In the intimate circle of the lodge, smoking the pipe of peace as a blessing for each prayer, I felt the palpable sacredness of that interconnection in ways I had never felt before. I also felt a creeping humility overcome any sense I may have had that my divinity degree was the culmination of my spiritual training. Clearly another spiritual adventure was just beginning.

Many indigenous peoples, when they begin prayer or worship, invoke the presence of their ancestors, honoring all those who have come before, confessing from the start that we cannot possibly do this work of living and loving, building and feeding, growing and healing all by ourselves. We seek the wisdom and nourishing company of all who have gone before, and pray for the healing of all who will come after.

In the same spirit, the traditional Buddhist *Metta,* a prayer of loving kindness, is offered for the alleviation of suffering of all sentient beings

> *May all beings be healed.*
> *May all beings be at peace.*
> *May all beings be free from suffering.*

PRAYING FOR OUR FAMILY

When I lead retreats, I begin by asking those present to think of someone dear to them. I ask them to recall a particular person whose loving kindness startled them awake, whose gift inspired them to be strong or faithful, who offered bread when they were hungry, water when they were parched with thirst.

"I want to bring my grandfather into the circle," explains a young pediatrician. "He was always kind to me, never harsh. Whenever I walk into the room of a child in my care, I remember his gentle manner, and I feel him there with me."

A woman speaks up. "I would like to invite my aunt," she says. "I had pneumonia when I was a little girl, and I remember my aunt sitting by my bed for hours, just sitting there, singing to me, holding my hand. She could not heal my sickness, but her presence made me feel strong and safe. I would like to feel her by my side again." She is quiet, a tear slowly spills onto her cheek.

A parent recalls when his daughter was about six. He had been working hard, late hours, coming home depleted and troubled by the weight of working and raising a family. "One night I collapsed in a chair, and could barely speak. I was bone tired. My daughter climbed up on my lap, and stroked my head, and said, 'I love you, Daddy.' I can never forget the touch of her fingers in my hair, those few simple words. She changed my mood in an instant. I felt grateful and at peace." He paused, and added, "I would like to bring my daughter into the circle."

And so it goes, people inviting teachers, lovers, friends who held or loved them into the circle. Healing, like communion, is shared, sacred bread passed around life's altar from hand to hand, generation to generation. When we pray, we invite all these into the quiet sanctuary of "our" prayer.

The gift of prayer holds a hidden paradox: When we pray alone, centered and still, we begin to feel less lonely. We taste the quiet companionship of God, and recall deep connections that nourish and sustain us.

I belong to a circle of people who meet a few times each year to exchange stories from our journeys, to share our challenges and blessings. One year, Hafsat, a young member of our group, was absent. She had been detained in her home country in Africa. No one knew when, or if, she would be allowed to leave. The previous government had killed her mother, and her father had died a political prisoner. We did not know what would happen to her, and we were afraid.

It was the night of her twenty-fifth birthday. She had always been a light in our circle, and in her sudden absence we ached from the missing of her company. While some of us were doing what little we could through connections at the State Department, we were essentially powerless, troubled and uncertain, not knowing what to do or say. For the most part, we could only wait.

Late in the evening, on the way to our respective rooms, several of us found ourselves spontaneously forming a circle on a path under the stars. As we held one another, we prayed aloud for her safe return. Amshatar, one of our circle, taught us an old African song that Hafsat's mother sang to her when she was small. It had always made Hafsat feel at peace in her mother's love.

And so, in a circle on a path in the Michigan woods, a small group of devoted friends prayed and sang a song that we knew, somehow, was the right song:

> *One person*
> *is not a good thing.*
>
> *One person*
> *is certainly not*
> *a good thing.*
>
> *O Lord,*
> *please do not make me*
> *one person.*

On the night of her twenty-fifth birthday, we sang to Hafsat under the cool brilliance of the night sky, so that wherever she was, she would not feel like one person, not alone, not this night.

PRAYER CONNECTS US WITH EVERYONE AND EVERYTHING

Our every word, thought, and action ripples into the world. Every step we take fertilizes the soil in which our children will plant their hopes and dreams. Every prayer we pray shapes the world for those who come after. And so before we speak, we must listen. What would benefit us all? What healing, if it came, would bring grace to both my loved ones and to me? When I pray for the healing of this cancer, this loneliness, this grief, I also pray for the healing of all who share my sorrow.

Swami Venkatesananda reminds us, "Any persons whom you have ever met, even if you have just exchanged a glance on a bus, have become part of your being, and consequently you are in some sense ultimately responsible for them. You carry them in your heart." When we commence our prayer with the word

Our, we open our hearts and the whole world spills out before us. Here, we begin to realize that to pray is no small thing. It is nothing less than a sacred pilgrimage into the heart of the whole world.

Prayer Practice

Prayer is a doorway into heaven on earth. It can open and clear our eyes and ears, quicken our heart, and deepen our mindfulness, so that we may more easily discern where heaven lives in this moment, in this place.

Although I often sit in my room and pray in front of my altar—a small table with candles, a few precious photographs, gifts from loved ones, and objects sacred to me—I just as often pray when I walk, allowing the cadence of my step to accompany my prayers.

However you pray, it is useful to retreat to a quiet place without distraction or responsibility. As you integrate prayer into your daily life, allow your prayers to gently find their place in you, in their own way, in their own time. Simply use the rhythm of your breathing to calm the incessant jumble of thoughts and worries, and anchor your sense of presence in the body, here, in this moment, in this place.

As you begin your prayer with this single word, *Our,* you may wish to ask yourself this question: With whom am I praying? You may imagine inviting someone you love to sit beside you in prayer, perhaps a person who has brought you sanctuary and comfort. Perhaps you will invite more than one being, and find yourself encircled with the reassuring company of many loved ones.

You may also wish to invite into your prayers the company of all beings who stand in need of care, the children of the world, the creatures of the earth. We can even call on the entire host of heaven to pray with us.

As you sit quietly, imagine that the yearnings of your heart are like seeds that germinate slowly in the soil of time. There is no need for hurry. As you name all the true and secret things that need to be spoken, imagine that this is *our* prayer, to *our* God. You may also invite into your circle those who are in need of some particular comfort, healing, or care. These may be loved ones who are facing illness or loss, or may include the poor and hungry, or those who suffer violence or war. As you invite those for whom your heart feels compelled to pray, *imagine we are all praying together for ourselves and for the healing of the world.*

REMEMBER THIS:
When we pray, we never, ever pray alone.

FATHER

We are beloved children of
a loving Creator, sons and daughters of
a Mother-Father God.

The word *Father* is perhaps, for many, the most troublesome word in this prayer. First, it implies that God is male. Second, because we inherit a theology traditionally interpreted through the eyes and ears of Western European men, we are saturated with images of God as a dramatically bearded, old, white male.

These habitual perceptions of the Divine, the Great Spirit, as an exclusively masculine force call up images of a dominant, controlling patriarch. They seem to imply that the more feminine aspects of the Divine—compassion, wisdom, tenderness, and patience—are somehow left out.

Our Father sounds as if we are choosing to worship a Father instead of a Mother. And yet it is impossible that God, the Creator of all things, would not contain and reflect the most nourishing aspects of both the masculine and the feminine. Native Americans pray to Father Sky and Mother Earth; Hindus worship Ram and Sita; many indigenous peoples honor both god and goddess, male and female aspects of the divine spirit. If God is the author of us all, then this loving, watchful Creator must be Father and Mother, Sister and Brother. Julian of Norwich says, "Just as God is truly our Father, so also is God truly our Mother." Even the conservative apostle Saint Paul admits it is a mistake to limit our understanding of the Divine to a single gender. "In Christ," he says, "there is neither male nor female."

When we open our deepest heart to God, the word *Father* may also trigger a more delicate, personal discomfort among those who have been wounded by their own fathers. What of the countless children who were abused in some intimate way by violent fathers? What of those abandoned or rejected by troubled, unkind fathers? Can Jesus really expect us to pray to such a "Father" and still feel safe and loved? This is impossible.

So why does Jesus choose this word, *Father*? Clearly he has other names at his disposal—Creator, Almighty, God—all of which would be acceptable ways to address the Divine. Yet Jesus deliberately chooses *Father* to set the tone for this prayer. Why?

PRAYER AS INTIMATE RELATIONSHIP

To understand Jesus' choice of language, we must recall that in the first century, the traditional gods of the Roman occupation were guardians of the state.

Greek and Roman gods were remote, far removed from the daily experiences of the people, and appeased more out of habit than devotion. They seemed to toy with humans for their own pleasure; indeed, the culture was replete with stories of gods haphazardly intervening in human affairs, capturing maidens and starting wars, and then betting on the outcome. People were the playthings of the gods, not intimately related to them in a caring, loving way.

Even in Jesus' own Judaic tradition, certain factions had taken over the management of the temple; ordinary men and women were banned from entering the *sanctum sanctorum,* the "holy of holies." Complex rules prescribed sacrifices that each family had to make to the priests, who were the only ones allowed to intercede on their behalf before God. In addition, many of Jesus' followers had been slaves, or worked as poor farmers or tradespeople for the Roman procurator. So the idea of being in direct, intimate relationship with the creator of the world was absolutely unthinkable. For ordinary people, God had become unapproachable.

Those who listened to Jesus lived in a time when their children were often born only to die, crops were planted and failed, people were oppressed and imprisoned, and war and famine were relentless companions. People ached for the loving company of an intimate God who knew them, who cared how they lived and whether they died. Who wept when their children succumbed to illness, who stood by them when they were afraid and lost. This was the God that Jesus called "Father," a God that looked after every one of them with a watchful, loving heart.

Jesus' radical stance was this: *Anyone can enter the household of heaven and speak directly with God.* The province of God is within us, right here, right now, in our midst. God is not just in the temple but here in the heart, in the children, in the wheat, in the wind, in the bread of life, in the love we share with one another. God is here, now, and loves us as deeply and intently as a parent loves their one and only child.

Jesus told them, *Not a sparrow falls without your heavenly Father knowing of it.* This was a God who was mindful of every earthly sadness and grieved every passing life. *Your heavenly Father knows the number of hairs on your head,* said Jesus, so closely does the Creator watch over your life.

So Jesus chooses the word *Father* not to distinguish God from *Mother,* but to challenge the concept of a God who is unavailable and unapproachable. Jesus uses the Aramaic word *Abba,* which is literally translated as "Daddy" or "Papa." Clearly Jesus is not addressing some cold and distant patriarch; he is invoking the company of an intimate and loving creator, to whom we belong in the deepest possible way.

WE ARE BELOVED CHILDREN OF A LOVING CREATOR

Before Jesus began his public ministry he presented himself to John the Baptist, who was baptizing spiritual seekers in the Jordan River. Baptism was a ritual cleansing, a symbolic rebirth into a new, spiritual life. This ritual, traditional in many cultures, prepared the one baptized to undertake a spiritual pilgrimage, a vision quest, a new calling.

As John baptized Jesus, the water, fresh and cool, ran down Jesus' face and hair, and the gates of heaven opened above him. A spirit, appearing as a dove, descended upon him and a voice from heaven spoke: *"Behold, this is my child, in whom I am well pleased."*

Like Jesus, we are beloved children of a loving God. Every day we can, through prayer, listen more carefully to the voice that repeats again and again, *You are my beloved child, in whom I am well pleased.* There is nothing we must do to earn this love or to drink from this blessing. It is a gift, freely offered, a blessing from a loving parent to a beloved child.

Jesus invites us to pray *Our Father*, not as an affirmation of *gender*, but rather as a radical affirmation of *relationship*. No longer merely subjects of the divine king, we are now intimate members of the family, welcome at the family table. For those who have been denied access to the sacred and bountiful gifts of the earth, this is a spiritual windfall.

Which parent among you, Jesus asks us, *if your child asks for bread, will instead give them a stone? And if they ask for a fish, will you give them a serpent? And what if they ask you for an egg—will you respond by giving them a scorpion?* This loving God to whom we pray is a parent so very much in love with us, aching to give us life, always life, whenever possible, life, life, life. Can you feel this when you pray? If you can, says Jesus, the household of God will be yours.

Like any good parent, God knows what you need, even before you ask. So your prayer can become more spacious and open, and not merely a catalog of your various desires. In truth, you may not be clearheaded or wise enough even to know exactly what your life requires in this moment. Rather, with humility and surrender, *simply make it known that you are ready to receive.* Readiness is the fruit of prayer. I am ready—ready to be taught, ready to be fed, ready to be healed, ready to be at peace.

A GOD WHO KNOWS
AND LOVES US

When we pray, we imagine a God who feels like us, who sees and knows us as we are. The creation story in Genesis affirms that we are made in the image of the Creator, and so an African expects the Creator to have the characteristics of an African; a farmer will pray to a God who understands the perils and blessings of farming; the pregnant peasant seeks the reassuring company of a divine Mother who has borne and cared for an infant child. This is only natural. In the Maori version of the Lord's Prayer, taken from the New Zealand Prayer

Book, the word for *Father* is translated as "Eternal spirit, Earth-maker, Pain-bearer, Life-giver, Source of all that is and all that shall be, Father and Mother of us all, Loving God, who is in heaven."

When I lived with Maryknoll missionaries in the shantytown slums outside Lima, Peru, religious processions were common. One foggy morning in winter, carefully stepping around the broken glass, rubble, and open sewage—ever-present reminders of their station as the discarded refuse of the world—an enthusiastic crowd of villagers carried a statue of a Black Madonna on a large pallet. Dressed in colorful clothing and singing cheerfully of their love and devotion to the divine mother, they wound their way through the narrow streets, stopping again and again before this or that home or family, making sure not to slight anyone who craved her blessing.

This statue looked nothing at all like the paintings I had seen of Mary as a lovely young white European courtier. Here was a dark, simple woman, bedecked in vibrant color and flowers, an ocean of flowers, her beauty emanating from her simplicity, her love made strong in part by her intimate resemblance to those who carried her all day long, her presence blessing everyone and everything.

As we listen to the language of the Lord's Prayer, we gradually realize something simple and obvious: *This is a child's prayer.* When Jesus uses the Aramaic *Abba,* he is not only invoking a deeply loving parent. He is invoking the child in us. We take refuge in our remembered smallness, daughters and sons awaiting the boundless kindness of a loving parent.

We must not allow a painful and corrosive dualism to force us to choose between Father and Mother. When we allow "Abba" to become more spacious, more feminine, expansive, and kind, we settle into a place where a truly loving Mother-Father God is a gift of divine love.

Prayer Practice

Can you imagine a presence so intimate that it actually lives in your own heart, where your sorrows are God's sorrows, and your dreams are God's dreams for you? If you can be still and feel the truth of this, you can surrender into the loving arms of your beloved protector.

When we address the divine spirit in prayer, we can speak with a familiar and comfortable intimacy. It is useful to lift up an image of a wise and loving elder, one who sees and loves us just as we are, one who feels strong and safe.

When we pray, we lean on the everlasting arms of God. Grant yourself permission to investigate different images that, for you, evoke feelings of nourishment and sanctuary. What images come to mind? Mother? Father? A loving teacher or mentor? Perhaps the Holy Spirit, or some other image of divine love? When you pray, take refuge in this image. Allow yourself to rest without words, settling into the comfort of unconditional love and acceptance.

From this place, deep and genuine prayer can begin. There is little to say or ask for, except: *Mother, Father, I am ready to receive your healing love and care.*

WHO ART IN HEAVEN

Heaven is everywhere, in everything,

in every moment.

We need only open our hearts to find it.

As we focus our awareness on this phrase, we may wonder: Where shall we find this *heaven* into which Jesus invites us? Is it a geographical location, a Garden of Eden found on some secret map? Is it somewhere in the sky, beyond the clouds, filled with the sound of harps and the songs of seraphim, bounded by luminous, pearly gates?

When Jesus described heaven, he never spoke of a place; rather, he described a state of the heart, a way of being attentive to the sacred in ordinary things, things we might easily overlook. He said that if we are awake and present, heaven can be found in such small things, like a mustard seed: You know the mustard seed, how small it is? If you drop it on the ground by mistake you may lose it. But if you place it carefully in the earth and give it water, a little time and care—then you see how it grows by itself into this beautiful bush, lush and full. The birds of the air come, build nests in its large branches, and sing. Oh, he said, heaven is just like that.

Then he would say, You know what heaven is like? It is a feeling you have perhaps when, in a warm kitchen on a winter's afternoon, you mix flour and water into dough for making bread. You take just a pinch of yeast, knead the leaven into the dough, and feel the warmth, the texture of the dough in your hands. Then you shape it, set it aside, and let it rest—and it rises all by itself. As it rises, you can feel, Oh, heaven is like this. Just like this.

Then he would add, Do you want to feel the shape of heaven? Heaven is like a pearl of great price, or a treasure hidden in a field. It is as when you have something so precious and beautiful, some delight or blessing that when you hold it in your hand, in that very moment, even if you never owned anything else, you would still be happy. Heaven feels just like that.

HEAVEN LIVES ON EARTH

For Jesus, heaven is a way of being gratefully awake every day upon the earth. Heaven is already here, in the bread we bake, the seeds we plant, the small blessings we receive. Thich Nhat Hanh, the beloved Vietnamese Buddhist monk, says that some of us wait for heaven after death. He advises us instead to remain fully awake and alive today, in this moment:

> There are some people who believe that they will enter the Kingdom of God, or the Pure Land, after they die. I don't agree with them. I know that you don't have to die in order to get into the Kingdom of God. *In fact, you have to be alive to do so.*

Many spiritual traditions have stories about heaven. There is a Vietnamese tale that contrasts heaven and hell. In hell, everyone is given an abundance of food, and then given chopsticks that are a yard long. Each person has all the food they need, but because the chopsticks are too long, they cannot bring the food to their mouths, and they all go hungry.

In heaven, the setting is exactly the same: Everyone is given an abundance of food, and their chopsticks are also a yard long. But in heaven, the people use their chopsticks to feed one another.

A single act of compassion can transform hell into

heaven. There is a Zen story in which a large, tough samurai went to see a little monk. "Monk," he said, in a voice accustomed to instant obedience, "teach me about heaven and hell!"

The monk looked up at this warrior and replied with utter disdain, "Teach you about heaven and hell? I couldn't teach you about anything. You're dirty. You smell. Your blade is rusty. You're a disgrace, an embarrassment to the samurai class. Get out of my sight, I can't stand you."

The samurai was furious. He shook, turned red in the face, and was speechless with rage. He pulled out his sword and raised it, preparing to slay the monk. At that instant the monk shouted, "Stop!" The samurai paused, shaking with murderous energy. "That," said the monk softly, "is hell."

The samurai was overwhelmed. He realized the compassion of this little man who was willing to sacrifice his life to offer him this teaching about hell. He put down his sword and felt a tearing in his heart. He lay down, placed his head in the lap of the little monk, and wept.

"And this," the monk said softly, "is heaven."

We can move from hell to heaven, or from heaven to hell, in an instant. Haven't we all felt that shift, when the heart quickly hardens, or is suddenly broken open? When we pray, we listen for that place where heaven is already alive, possible and present within us, in this moment, in this very breath. We feel the leaven in the bread, already kneaded into our life. All we need to do is hold it in our hands, and feel it rise.

THE BLESSING OF SMALL THINGS

When we settle in to pray, we often approach our prayer time tired, overworked, and exhausted. There is a nameless ache, a worry that we do not have what we need in order to be happy and at peace. Perhaps we feel ashamed that we are not doing our best, not offering our love and kindness very skillfully to our kin and community. When we pray, we may feel the frantic pace of busyness and overwork that does insidious violence to our soul. And this violence may create a persistent sadness that needs to be named, to be spoken aloud, to be seen and heard.

When bone-weariness runs this deep, prayer can seem an act far too feeble to fully transform our despair. How can something so small and quiet heal anything? Maybe we are convinced we need stronger medicine, something more powerful and dramatic to lift us up and rescue us from our weary disappointments.

But Jesus said, *If you are faithful in the small things, you will be faithful in the large things.* Every parent knows that our most potent interventions are in the small things: the wiped nose, the sweater hastily fastened before a child runs into the cold, the cup of hot chocolate upon her return. Heaven is born in this world, the small world of a good word, a kind touch, a loving glance, a moment of tender understanding. When we think of heaven, it need not be dramatic, grandiose, or even visible. Rather, prayer invites us to look for what is small, the gentle rising and falling of the breath, a sip of wine and piece of bread, a prayer uttered quietly without hurry.

David is a junior high school teacher. When he was a boy, he was fond of throwing stones. One afternoon, he discovered that if he tossed stones over his neighbor's fence, he could create a crashing sound, the sound of breaking glass. So he would heave a stone, and wait for the crash. Heave, crash. It was great fun. It felt a little dangerous—he might get caught, after all—but that, to a small boy, was part of the excitement.

As it happened, he did get caught. One day, the man who lived next door came to his house and told his parents about the boy and the stones. "I would like David to come to my home, so I can show him a few things," the man said, in a tone David took to be quite ominous. His parents, ashamed of and disappointed by their son's behavior, readily sent their son to the neighbor's house.

David sheepishly followed the man into his house, through the back door, and out into the yard. There, next to the fence David was so fond of throwing rocks over, was a greenhouse. The stones had shattered many panes of glass. Once whole, the greenhouse now looked wounded, defeated. As the man led David into the greenhouse, David, imagining all manner of punishments, felt he was going straight to hell. What was the man going to do to him?

Carefully stepping over scattered shards of broken glass, the neighbor led David down the rows of plants and began talking about flowers. He took David slowly, showing him each one and explaining what he loved about them. "These," he said, "are my gladiolas. They can get quite large, and bloom in many colors. These are violets, they were my wife's favorite. When I see them, I remember her, and I miss her. In the deep purple, she still lives in my eyes. And these orchids, right here, are very difficult to grow. But when they bloom, they create the most exquisite shapes and textures. You cannot believe until you see with your own eyes how a flower can be so beautiful."

David was shocked. There was no lecture, no beating, no punishment at all. After about an hour of showing David everything he loved about his flowers, and the greenhouse that helped him to grow them, the neighbor thanked David for coming, and told him he was free to go. As he walked home, David strangely felt as if he had been in heaven.

"At that moment," David told me, "I knew I would grow up and be a teacher. This man had done a very small thing—he showed me what he loved. He could have yelled about the glass, punished me for being destructive. But instead he took a few thoughtful minutes to share with me the fragrances and colors that meant so much to him. In a single hour, that man changed the course of my entire life."

Jesus is clearly telling us not to look *up* to find heaven, but rather to look *inward. The kingdom is within you,* said Jesus. It is as close as your breath, as close as your children, as close as the touch of a loved one, as close as the earth beneath your feet, the lilies in the field, the violets in the greenhouse, or the bread in your mouth. Here, we taste the blessing of Teresa of Avila: "All the way to heaven is heaven."

Prayer Practice

At retreats, I often ask people to imagine: What is the smallest thing anyone ever did for you or gave you that brought you significant healing or comfort? After a few moments of reflection, a flood of memories fills the room.

A minister, weary at the end of a very long day, visited a sick girl in the hospital. She said, "You look tired. I think you need an angel." So she drew him a picture of a heart with angels in it, and thanked him for coming.

A grandmother whose husband passed away last year recently found a letter he wrote her when he was dying, a letter she did not know about, which he hid in such a way that she would find it after he was gone. In it, he tells her how much he still loves her, and says he is with her always.

Christine, an art therapist, was working with Sophia, a critically ill girl in the hospital. One afternoon, Christine stopped a busy surgeon in the hall and suggested he give Sophia some kind of present before he performed a delicate and risky procedure on her the next day. The surgeon, hurried and obviously annoyed, mumbled something about being overwhelmed and stomped off. The next morning, as Sophia was being wheeled into surgery, Christine spied a small teddy bear in her arms, a secret gift from the surgeon.

When people share a memory of some small gesture that healed them, it is always from someone who listened, someone who was present and attentive, someone who simply saw them as they were. The keys of heaven turn on the smallest of things. An hour in a greenhouse, a kind letter, a teddy bear, a picture of angels.

Recall one small thing that has brought you healing or comfort. When you pray, allow your heart to rest on this precious, single moment. When we pray in the company of even the smallest of blessings, the doors of the household of heaven are thrown wide open.

HALLOWED BE THY NAME

When we pray, we stand on holy ground;
we consent to be surprised by
a rich and sacred mystery.

At this point in the prayer, we encounter two ancient questions. First: *What is holy?* And second: *What is the name of God?*

It is said that something is holy when it has been set apart from the ordinary, the purely material, the profane. When we imagine holy things we may think of a cross, a cathedral, a mosque, a statue of the Buddha. But what makes something holy?

Frank Waters was a gifted author, legendary for his sensitive explorations of Native American spirituality. He put this very question to me in his home, when he was near the end of a rich, full life. "Do you believe things are sacred in themselves," he asked, "or are they made sacred when we consecrate them with our attention?" This was no trick or riddle, but an earnest inquiry emerging from a lifetime of living with a people who held land and mountain, corn and sun, as sacred, holy things.

He wondered, for example, if Taos Mountain—visible through his small, blue-framed window, and long revered by the people of Taos Pueblo as sacred—was essentially holy in itself, or, rather, was made holy through the worship and devotion offered by countless generations of loving people in the valley. It was a conversation punctuated by long pauses and deep silence. In the end, we could only conclude that there must live in all things some deep conversation, an intricate relationship of mutual blessing, where both mountain and people bless one another, and in the soil of that loving relationship something truly holy is born.

So just as the cross, the mosque, and the images of the Buddha or the Virgin of Guadalupe are all holy, so are we made holy by our devotion to them. We call this relationship "con-secration"—literally, "to make holy together." Holiness arises out of this mutual blessing when we are in loving, respectful relationship with what we hold sacred.

DISCOVERING THE SACRED
WITH A BEGINNER'S MIND

How do we honor the holiness in things? The psalmist says, *I lift up my eyes unto the hills, from whence cometh my help.* In the Catholic mass, we say, *Lift up your hearts; we lift them up to the Lord.* When we lift our eyes to see a hawk, lazy and still in an impossibly blue sky; when we lift our eyes to see the colors of fall, a double rainbow, a magnificent sunset, we shift our attention from the relentless seductions of obligation and detail, and consent to be surprised by holiness anywhere, and everywhere.

As the Buddhist teacher Suzuki Roshi reminds us, "In the beginner's mind there are many possibilities. In the expert's mind there are few." Once we become experts, we feel we can stop paying close attention. We know what is coming, we have seen it all before. We go a little bit to sleep. But when we are beginners, everything is fresh and new, each moment an adventure of discovery, every act contains a promise of surprise.

When we pray *Hallowed be thy name,* we always come as beginners. When we set off in search of heaven, we begin an endless adventure. We consistently encounter intimate relationships with things not readily

43

understood by ordinary thought. We surrender to a magnificent mystery where anything is possible.

The ways of the Divine are vast and spacious. When we pray, we feel very small in the presence of very large things; who knows what will be given, what will be required? In prayer, we consent to remain present and awake, to be open to however holiness arises. When we pray in the company of such deep mystery, all we can honorably offer is this: *I am here. I am yours. Hear my prayer.*

THE ESSENCE OF GOD IS A MYSTERY

When we pray *Hallowed be thy name,* we honor what is holy, and we lift up the name of the Divine. But Jesus mentions no specific name for God. The names of God are legion: Wakan Tankha, Vishnu, Jehovah, Allah, Quan Yin, Adonai, Shiva—hundreds, thousands of names, reflecting countless aspects of the Divine. But Jesus does not single out any one; he does not say, Hallowed be Yahweh, or Adonai, Lord God Almighty. He does not name God because, as a Jew, he knows the Divine is nameless.

In the scripture Jesus studied as a child, God appeared to Moses in the form of a burning bush. "What is your name?" Moses asked. And God answered Moses, "I AM WHO I AM. Say this to the people of Israel: I AM has sent me to you."

Of all the glorious names for the Divine—King of Kings, Great Spirit, Allah, Mother Goddess—to say only "I am who I am" seems simple and honest. The Jews never spoke God's name aloud, recognizing that any name makes God too small. Some Jewish scholars prefer "I will be who I will be." Here, there is a sense of God unfolding and evolving by our side, discovered in a thousand unexpected revelations. With such a name, God can be discovered anywhere.

All scripture is a treasure of stories collected, in the end, to paint a picture of the nature of God. There is no single name large enough, and so we tell everything, every moment where God is seen, felt, tasted. What can we possibly leave out? The list is too long; it takes an entire human life just to say it.

CALLING OUT TO GOD

When we are frightened, when we have been given a cancer diagnosis, when we have lost something precious, a job, a lover, a child—to whom do we call out in our grief? When we cry aloud the name of God, who do we hope will answer?

At this point in prayer, we wait in silence for the mystery to reveal itself. We bow before what cannot be spoken. The nature of God is infinite and unspeakable, as unfathomable as the countless wounds and blessings that confound our hearts. In silent prayer, we may find there are things in us so powerful, so deep, they cannot be named at all. What words can possibly hold the immensity of our sorrow, the ache of heart and weariness of bone? What sound can we make that can express our yearning for peace, for release, for healing? A heart broken is not so easily repaired with words, so we stumble a little, fumble for the right way to say what can never be said.

Perhaps this is why much of our prayer gently melts into silence. We pray that this mysterious, loving, Mother-Father presence can hear what we cannot possibly say, as a parent knows by the way a child's face changes that they are in need of holding, of protection. No words are necessary; something larger than ourselves plumbs our depths, hears what is named in silence, and responds.

Hallowed be thy name. Here, we bow to what is infinite and eternal. We bow before what we can never fully comprehend. We bow to all the wisdom and healing in the universe. We bow to forces larger than ourselves. We bow to the Creator of our life, and all life. We bow before the holy mystery.

Prayer Practice

We often seek desperately for God when we are thrust into uncertainty. What once seemed secure and reliable now feels unstable and uncomfortable. Our relationship to ourselves, to the world, and to God is unclear, and we ache for the familiar comfort and safety of knowing where we are, and where we are going.

In prayer, we reach out to the stable anchor of God, a place to stand on shifting ground. We can use *Hallowed be thy name* as a simple prayer that reassures us that the essential nature of God is always present and available to us.

So when we pray *Hallowed be thy name,* we also pray *May we feel the comforting presence of God in our confusion and uncertainty. May we recognize the footprint of God's companionship even when we are lost and afraid. May we take refuge in the unchanging essence of God, as our nourish-ment and our sanctuary.*

Using this phrase to punctuate every act, we invoke the invisible mystery of heaven embedded in the visible and the ordinary. We consecrate our every action with our prayer.

We light a candle. *Hallowed be thy name.*

We see the sun set in brilliant crimson. *Hallowed be thy name.*

We gather with loved ones. *Hallowed be thy name.*

We offer a word of kindness. *Hallowed be thy name.*

We sit in silence. *Hallowed be thy name.*

THY KINGDOM COME

We are always welcome
in the household of God.

The phrase *Thy kingdom come* invokes two distinctly different prayers. Imagine two chambers of the heart, sending and receiving blood in life-giving rhythm, giving out and taking in. This prayer, likewise, sends and receives faith, hope, and love in the deep rhythmicity of the heart.

The first beat of this prayer, the sending out, expresses our thirst for the kingdom of heaven. *We are in need: May thy kingdom come.* When we are lost, when we are sick, bereft, frightened, lonely, we ache for our loving Creator to come, to be close, to be with us and bring us courage, wisdom, healing, and peace. We cry out for the comfort of heaven, the balm of Gilead, the cup that runneth over, the full measure of love and healing promised us, without condition, as children of a loving Creator.

The second beat of the prayer cries out to receive, to be awakened to all those places where the kingdom of heaven has already been given us. *Thy kingdom has come; open my eyes that I may see it.* We have been given everything we need—strength and nourishment to heal, wisdom and courage to be clear and wise. We cry out for eyes to see, for ears to hear, where heaven is everywhere, alive within us this very moment.

WE ARE IN NEED; MAY THY KINGDOM COME

When we pray, confessing our tender yearnings to a loving Creator, the word *kingdom* can feel harsh and intrusive to our modern ears. Why does Jesus use it?

Jesus' listeners believed that the power of the Creator would manifest as a kingly principality, with God on a mighty throne, governing heaven and earth. Unfortunately, this image has proved an irresistible ally for countless warriors throughout history. People and nations have greedily appropriated this kingly image of God to fight for their cause, to justify war, pillage, and plunder, to bring the kingdom of God to earth to serve their own particular religious and political desires.

But for Jesus it is clear *kingdom* means something completely different. In Jesus' kingdom, all are welcome—the poor, the unclean, the sinners, prostitutes, and tax collectors. Jesus throws open the doors, inviting all who feel left out, welcoming anyone, anywhere, to come to the table and be fed. It is more accurate to translate the word *kingdom* as *household*, a joining together of people for the good of all. *Household* is a word found in early Jewish scripture that describes a place where everyone can find sanctuary, nourishment, and care. Here, *Thy kingdom come* may just as rightly be prayed: *May we be welcome in the household of God.*

YEARNING FOR THE KINGDOM

I worked for several years in southern California with young gang members and their families. I spent many days and nights in neighborhoods, in homes, around kitchen tables, listening for where the seeds of peace and reconciliation might be buried in the ground of violence, payback, and terror. There was a disturbing presumption of death, something always close, in the air, never completely out of mind. In communities regularly disregarded by their more affluent neighbors, there ripened the inevitable fruits of economic and political impotence; violence and rage, warfare over scraps of territory, even murder became commonplace tools to secure temporary dominion over diminishing crumbs.

On the altar of this landscape, children were the sacrificial offerings. I became very close to the Romeros, a devout Catholic family who had two sons. At St. Mary's, I joined them and the community to pray the rosary over the body of Ramon, aged nineteen, who had been killed for standing on the wrong side of the wrong argument. The neighborhood gathered, as they had far too many times, to listen to the words, ancient and barely comforting, warming their hearts around the promise of hope and healing not yet come. *Hail Mary, full of grace . . . Our Father, who art in heaven . . . Thy kingdom come.* Here, in this place, around this altar, we cried out for the kingdom of heaven to come, for some kind of justice to visit this place, for some peace, some miracle of well-being to flow like a river from the heart of Mary, from the heart of God, to wash this place clean of sorrows beyond counting, beyond naming.

Immediately Ramon's little brother, Jimmy, vowed

to avenge Ramon's death. In spite of all my counsel, my skilled (or so I imagined, in my youthful ignorance and grandiosity) interventions, my visits with his family, Jimmy would not be dissuaded from what he believed was his duty, his sacred vow to square his brother's account. And so when Jimmy died, underneath a car, having crawled there after taking a bullet in his back, we said the rosary again. *Hail Mary, full of grace . . . Thy kingdom come.* Again and again, here and in a thousand places every day, families and communities gather to pray for the coming of the kingdom, for the peace that will heal what has been broken, for the justice that will make right what we have made so terribly wrong.

SEEKING THE HOUSEHOLD
OF HEAVEN

When we are given something that we cannot bear, we pray for a kind hand to lighten the load, to take away the burden we have been given. When Brian was first diagnosed with AIDS in 1987, he wept in my arms. At twenty-seven, he was young, vital, and creative. But in those early days, when AIDS brought swift and certain death, Brian pleaded with forces larger than himself.

Why me? Why is God punishing me? Oh please, please don't make me die. When Paul was dying of cancer, after three rounds of excruciating radiation and chemotherapy, he told me he prayed every day for the blessing, however unimaginable, of just a few hours free from his relentless, life-sapping pain.

In these stories we hear an echo of Jesus at Gethsemane, on the night he was to be arrested, and the next day tortured, and killed. *Abba, Abba, I do not wish to die. If it be thy will, please, please take this cup from me.* . . . Even Jesus, in his loneliest of moments, deserted by all who loved him, prayed for the blessed relief of the kingdom of heaven to come, to relieve him of his unbearable sorrow and suffering.

When we center ourselves and listen to the wishes of our heart, we pray that the kingdom of peace and healing will, in some palpable way, enter into our lives. *Take this cup from me. Deliver me from this illness. Grant my children joy and strength. Keep me safe. Grant me wisdom. Show me the way. Heal me. Grant us peace.*

The arrival of the kingdom will feel different for each of us, and it will change with time, age, and circumstance. When our children are sick, the only kingdom we can imagine is one in which our children are

54

strong and healthy once again. When we are lost or painfully confused in our life, relationship, or career, we pray for a kingdom where we know our way and can feel our sense of place and belonging. If we are lonely, we ache for a kingdom where we are seen and known, held and loved by others. When we are in conflict, we yearn for peace. When we are thirsty, we pray for water. When we are hungry, God can only come in the form of food.

And so we pray: *May thy kingdom come. May the household of heaven be open and welcoming.* We light candles and beseech the Spirit to descend upon us. We perform invocations, we call out in the wilderness for companionship and healing. When we enter a sanctuary, church, cathedral, synagogue, ashram, sweat lodge, we can feel the silent resonance of every prayer ever spoken, all the silent pleadings of troubled hearts that saturate the atmosphere. We bask in the lingering fragrance of candles, incense, and sage that carry the heart's cry into heaven. When we are quiet and still, we listen for the place where all will be well, and all manner of things shall be well.

THY KINGDOM HAS COME; OPEN MY EYES THAT I MAY SEE HEAVEN ON EARTH

My friend Elizabeth has a daughter, Melody, who is ten years old. She told me that while they were walking together in a park, a loose dog unexpectedly charged Melody, knocked her over, and bit her. The dog's teeth cut clear through her hand, resulting in a gruesome confusion of mangled tendon, bone, and tender flesh. After rushing Melody to the hospital, Elizabeth prayed for healing, for some healing grace to comfort her hurt and frightened little girl.

After a seemingly endless series of treatments and surgeries, and with the skillful care of nurses, doctors, and physical therapists, Melody's hand began to get better. At the same time, Elizabeth noticed Melody was abnormally quiet, somehow turned in to herself. She rarely spoke, and never about her hand or the dog. Elizabeth, concerned for Melody's inner state, kept asking her daughter how she was feeling. "I have nightmares" was all Melody could offer, returning to silence.

Elizabeth shared her worry about Melody with a social worker who began to visit several times a day just to sit with her, quietly, without agenda or expectation. After a week or so she asked Melody about the dog, and her hand. Slowly, reluctantly, Melody offered a word, a phrase, finally a sentence or two about what had happened, what she remembered, how it felt. She wept at the telling of it.

Soon Melody was able to share more of her story, adding more detail, telling her mother, the nurses, family members, anyone who would listen. As the hidden memories emerged and found the attention of loving ears, the nightmares decreased. After a few weeks, they stopped completely. The story had been fully told; now the grace, unexpectedly hidden within the wound, could be released to do its good and healing work.

The healing we so desperately seek may already be embedded within the wound itself. The gift of peace comes only when we acknowledge the wounds of war. While we pray for God's healing presence, we also pray to see, hear, feel, and taste where the Spirit is already hidden in our trouble. Jesus says that heaven is everywhere, always, as close as our breath: *The kingdom of God is already here. It is within you and among you. You are the light of the world. You are already blessed. The field is already white with harvest. If your eye is clear, your body will be full of light. If you have eyes, let them see; if you have ears, let them hear.*

If this is true, if we believe what he says, then, having

petitioned the Spirit for our wants and needs, we can allow our prayer to gently shift. We pray not so much for the outside world to change, but for our eyes to be opened, our faith to be quickened, for our inner peace to come alive. *May our hearts be open, may our souls be awake, may we receive the healing that is already here, in this moment.*

In the Gospel of Mark, Jesus' first recorded teaching describes this ever-present kingdom. *The time is full, and the kingdom of heaven is here. Be awake, be changed, and taste the goodness of it.* Jesus is quite clear: The kingdom has already come. Not in the future in some faraway place, not in some eventual destination, not as a reward for all your tireless efforts, but offered freely, right here, right now.

ENTERING THE HOUSEHOLD OF HEAVEN

In our hurried, worry-filled lives, we usually feel time is running out. But for Jesus, time is filling up. *The time is full, and the kingdom of heaven is here.* When we are preoccupied with our work, our accomplishments, and our acquisitions, when we are desperate to get and to achieve, we miss the blessings already present, the ridiculously abundant signs of heaven that surround us, if we are only the slightest bit awake. As we walk, lost in the seductive chaos of our weighty concerns, we will pass by the willow and the rose, the dandelion and the tulip, the forsythia and the lilac without *seeing,* without being aware of anything but the dense muddle of our own preoccupations. We will ignore the jasmine and the honeysuckle, the playful surprise of clouds and the impossibly brilliant colors of the sky.

I have been granted the privilege to accompany countless women and men, families, children, and communities who have struggled with all manner of human suffering. Without fail, as we listen together for the hidden groundwater of healing, we find some poignant mixture of both sorrow and grace.

The first thing we see—the experience that invariably presents itself with the most dramatic flourish—is the unbearable, the unspeakable, the sorrow deeper than words. Cancer, alcoholism, incest, divorce, the death of a loved one, the corrosive loss of inner peace. Ten thousand sorrows, the Buddha said, is our inheritance when we take birth as human beings. Sometimes when we gather, it is these sorrows that bring us together.

But curiously, when we remain still and awake in

the country of sorrow, we invoke a gradual willingness to imagine a simultaneous emergence of grace, of some hidden wholeness. Sam Lewis, the beloved Sufi master, would often say, "It is not a matter of when you reach the kingdom of heaven. It is a matter of when the kingdom of heaven reaches you."

Turn your eye to heaven; do not miss it, do not be seduced by the enormity of sorrow. There is something greater, something that will not die, that refuses to be extinguished, regardless of the weight of anguish handed you. Put your heart on this. *Seek first the kingdom,* Jesus said, *and all the rest will be given to you.*

In hospice, we gather around the bedside of someone riddled with cancer or some other life-draining illness. As we sit together, feelings rise in us, and there is anger, and sadness; there is the changing of bed linens, finding the lip balm to moisturize parched lips, bending the straw to coax a few drops of liquid into the mouth, and the ache of unimaginable weariness. But at the very same moment, embedded in the sorrow or right next to it, there is this astonishing tenderness, unimaginable kindness, sweet honesty, tender patience, quiet generosity, and deep, abiding love. This does not make sense if the only thing born of sorrow is suffering. The other thing born is the kingdom, the grace, the doors flung open into the household of God.

SURPRISED BY HEAVEN

Last year my friend Soleil was bravely fighting a cancer that doctors, over a decade earlier, had insisted would kill her in a year. Through tireless research, limitless courage, an astonishing array of treatments combined with sheer stubbornness and will, Soleil had managed to outlive all her prognoses. But now she was dying. Though she would not admit it to herself or to anyone who loved her, we could not help but watch as her life began to slip out of her body.

One afternoon I took her to the doctor to have a catheter inserted, a painful, invasive procedure she hated and feared. While we waited, she asked me to hold her hand. So I sat beside her, and with one hand in hers, my other hand on her back, we sat together in silence, breathing, waiting. "Your hands are so warm," she said. "It makes me feel calm, more peaceful. Don't leave me," she pleaded. In the belly of this cancer, we had stumbled on an oasis of peace, a gentle fragrance of heaven.

A month later, my friend Diana and I were at Soleil's bedside as night fell in a hospital a hundred miles from our home. Soleil was waiting for yet another surgery, and there was little for us to do but wait with her. But Soleil was not a person to wait passively, so she asked us to sing to her. Diana and I demurred, fumbling excuses about not knowing exactly what to sing, but Soleil was not to be denied. At that moment a music therapist—a volunteer with a guitar and a songbook—appeared in the doorway, and asked, "Do you want to sing?"

In an instant we were thumbing through the song-book, and off we went, gleefully discovering old, for-gotten folk songs, ballads, hymns, and show tunes. Through the night we sang, passing the guitar from hand to hand, inventing harmonies, swimming in the unexpected music and company and hope that filled both the room and our hearts, something rooted in joy, right beneath something else just as certainly rooted in illness and death.

Two months later, at Soleil's memorial service, Diana and I sang one of the songs from that night as a tribute, in part to Soleil, and partly as tribute to the wonder of what refuses to die, some deep music that blows through us whenever we are willing and able to listen.

Look, says Jesus: *Keep your eyes on heaven.* You will

be given trial and tribulation, but you will also be given healing and grace. Watch the grace. The grace will not make the sorrow disappear; but neither will the sorrow eradicate the grace. *Seek first the kingdom;* listen for where heaven lives, come into the household of God. The kingdom has come. Let it become the altar of your heart's attention, and it shall be the star that will guide your way.

Prayer Practice

Prayer is an exquisite opportunity to be grateful. *The time is full, and the kingdom of heaven is here.*

Allow the mind to become still, and take a few moments to recall the gifts and blessings you may have overlooked in the rush and hurry of the day. Let them arise one at a time; take all the time you need to savor your life, your loved ones, your food and shelter, anyone who offered kindness or support, any nourishment or delight.

We may offer our blessing to each and every gift: blessings to the sun that warmed the day, blessings to my friends who accompanied me, blessings to this food that

nourished me, blessings to all who cared for me, blessings to all I met who were in need of care.

Every moment of our life can be a gift, a sign of the
kingdom come in our life. In prayer, we try to place our
heart's attention on every blessing we receive, each one
a precious jewel, a sign of the living presence of the
kingdom of God present today and always in our life.
When we saturate our prayer with such gratitude, we
open the door to a lightness of being, a fullness of spirit,
and enter the sweet household of heaven.

THY WILL BE DONE

*We are in loving hands; there are wise
and subtle forces that guide and
protect us every moment.*

There are plans, and there is life. I had planned, by the end of the week, to finish writing the first draft of this book. Instead, we had a big storm, the roof leaked, and I had to spend a day caulking seemingly endless fissures, leaks, and crannies. Then a close friend died suddenly in Los Angeles, and I used the rest of the week connecting with his friends and family, sharing loss and confusion, and helping to plan a memorial service. When I came back home, I had a parent's conference with my daughter's teacher. A week of writing had been transformed into days of rain, death, and children. And so go the days of a life on earth.

When we say *Thy will be done,* we acknowledge our willingness to enter into a profoundly intimate relationship with the loving Creator of the world, whose power and energy quicken and flow through all life. As we pray these words, we agree to respect the mystery of creation, to be attentive to the evolving presence of God, and to honor the movement of spiritual forces larger and wiser than ourselves as they guide and shape our lives.

When we pray—even in silence—we are speaking. And when we speak, we presume another is listening. We beseech, and wait for another to respond. Here is where prayer differs essentially from meditation. Meditation is a practice of cultivating a penetrating, mindful awareness of whatever can be observed in this moment. Prayer, on the other hand, presumes what the theologian Martin Buber calls an "I-Thou" relationship. We engage in a conversational, interactive covenant with another about how we wish things to be—while at the very same moment praying for the wisdom and courage to accept things as they are.

In any life, there are moments when we are confronted with some event or outcome we do not expect and surely do not want. In spite of doing our very best to raise our children well, to be successful in our work, to take care of our health, and to cultivate strong, loving relationships, to be faithful, good, and kind—in spite of our hopeful hearts, something goes wrong, something falls apart, we lose something precious, we become ill, or someone dies.

Here, the prayer *Thy will be done* becomes a litmus test of our faith. We not only confess that we are in relationship with some force greater than ourselves. We also humbly allow that this force—wise and loving, capable of seeing us and knowing us transparently and deeply—in spite of our will and our plans and our dreams, may ultimately know more than we do about what is best for us. There may be larger plans about which we are unaware, and we submit our will to be led, to be taught, to be shown what we did not wish to see and go where we did not wish to go.

This is the ground of prayer. First, we bring our deepest heart's desire to our loving Creator: Oh, God, take this cancer from me. Blessed Mary, please keep my children safe. Loving Creator, please grant me strength to achieve my goals. Allah, let there be honorable justice. Great Spirit, please let us be kind and wise in our dealings with our Mother, the earth. At each juncture we offer our hopes and yearnings for a world made right, peaceful, and whole.

And then our prayer shifts, and we declare our

willingness to let it be, to receive what we are given, to find peace and healing, whatever the outcome. To cultivate more than resignation; to cultivate acceptance, serenity, even gratitude for whatever seeds of wisdom, redemption, or liberation may be hidden in the unwanted challenges of the day.

WE PLACE OUR LIFE
IN LOVING HANDS

When Jesus was in the garden at Gethsemane, anticipating the horror of being arrested and tortured, he pleaded with his friends, *Will you please stay awake with me?* Despite their earnest promises, they all soon fell asleep. Not a single one remained awake to accompany him. Jesus prayed then to be liberated from his excruciating fate. *Father, if it be thy will, take this cup from me.*

But Jesus did not end with this anguished plea for deliverance from his suffering. He added a potent petition that defines the practice of prayer: *Nevertheless, not my will, but thine be done.*

This is the essence of prayer. The first part of prayer is the work we do each and every day, work with our hands and hearts to make the world safe and good, to heal those who are sick, to feed those who are hungry, to comfort those who are lonely, to create justice, to preserve the earth. Then, having brought our heart's desires and our offerings to the table, we prepare ourselves to gratefully receive whatever is given as a gift, a teaching offered by forces infinitely larger than ourselves, whose ways we may never fully comprehend.

Spiritual life is a life of surprise. We never get just the parts we want. When we are asked to accept something unexpected, when we are given something we had not sought or wanted, how do we meet it? Do we greet it with anger, frustration, impatience? Or do we welcome it as a gift, an opportunity to become more spacious, a dancing lesson from God?

Several years ago, I was very sick with near-fatal pneumonia. After a few weeks in the hospital, it was months before I fully regained my strength. Over time, I became impatient and frustrated with my inability to perform even the smallest tasks. Leaving my bed to prepare a simple meal left me exhausted for the rest of the day. I had been working at an AIDS clinic and there were patients to see; I was in charge of a local philanthropic organization and there were projects to visit and grants to dispense to those in need. Besides, I had my children who needed me. How long could they manage without my guidance and attention?

But stronger than my impatience was another sensation deep in the cells of my body, in my bones. When I lay back on my pillow and allowed myself to let go of all my responsibilities—both real and imagined—I fell into a palpable feeling of surrender. In the midst of this terrible illness, I sensed that somehow everything would be all right. It was not that I knew I would survive the pneumonia. Rather, I had a visceral awareness that regardless of what happened—even if I died, or if it took a very long time for me to be well—everything would, in some way, be all right. In the years since my recovery, I have never lost that feeling of trust in something fundamentally good and true that will bear me up in times of need. For many years after my recovery, my daily prayer was simply this: *Thy will be done.*

THY WILL FOR ME BE DONE

Last year I participated in a retreat, a circle of people who spent their lives fighting for human rights around the world. As part of their vocation they devoted their days to healing the torn bodies and hearts of children and adults who were summarily tortured because of their race, their ethnicity, or their beliefs. Some in our group had been tortured themselves.

Sequoyah, a Native American, convened this circle of all ages and nations. He began every session with the same prayer: *Creator, whatever it is you want me to do today, that is what I want to do. Whatever it is you want me to say, today, Creator, that is what I want to say. Wherever it is you want me to go today, Creator, that is where I want to go.*

This honest, humble prayer—essentially *Thy will be done,* repeated as a sacred chant of surrender—opened us up to be moved by the Spirit. In the midst of our plans and agendas, and our tasks to be accomplished by the end of our meeting, we suddenly left a great deal of room for the unexpected, the unlooked-for. We went around the circle, each taking our time with a talking stick. We went around the circle again and again for four days, in our meeting room, in pipe ceremonies, in the sweat lodge; round and round we went, discarding our expectations, trusting that whatever gifts arose within the circle would be precisely what we needed.

As the smoke of the pipe took our prayers heavenward, in the heat of the rocks in the sweat lodge, we prayed. We prayed with hesitancy and courage, weeping, racking sobs, injustices named and murders witnessed, shame confessed and courage found. There was a rich communion of silence punctuated by celebratory prayers of honest thanksgiving. Every word spoken in the circle was prayer, prefaced always by surrender: *Whatever you want me to say, Creator, that is what I want to say.*

Slowly, our conversation about human rights evolved into a collaboration about human responsibilities, how we might be with one another, what we owe one another—respect, honor, love, and care—and how we invite that into our lives, into our work, into the family of the earth. This was not the agenda we had brought; we had expected to formulate a statement, a plan, a time line. Instead we discovered the surprise of the Spirit at work within and among us, a force for healing alive and vital, from which we could drink and which we vowed to use in our peace-craft in the world. At the end of the retreat, I felt I had been shown a tangible manifestation of how potent *Thy will be done* can become when it is embraced in a circle of courageous, open hearts.

SURRENDER IN ORDINARY LIFE

My neighbor Susan was a postal worker. An injury to her hands forced her to quit her job. For years she went to doctors and healers hoping to get well, waiting for the day she could return to work. Her hands would get better and then worse, a torturous roller coaster of hope and discouragement. She planned on going back in three months, then six, then a year. She did odd jobs, temporary work to make ends meet, all the while waiting for her old life to resume.

Finally, she told me, "I realized I was being told, *Surrender, surrender, surrender.*" Now, after five years, she knows there is no going back, her life has been changed. She now waits differently, patiently waiting to be led by the Spirit. She works part-time, earning enough to survive, and with her free time she helps Nepalese refugees and raises money for immigrants and the oppressed. She never knows what each day will bring.

She also makes prayer flags and donates the profits to support Buddhist nuns and monks. One summer afternoon she came to tie a string of prayer flags in my backyard. Their beautiful colors dance in the breeze, and the wind takes their prayers. "Now," she said, "my prayer is simply to accept whatever is put before me. I don't waste time trying to figure out which is the best or most important thing to do; I just do what is given to me, from sewing prayer flags to taking out the garbage. Then I have no worries. This is my daily prayer. It has completely transformed my life."

A friend who flies hot-air balloons told me that when his balloon is tethered to the ground, being filled with air and readied for flight, the winds buffet the balloon and the basket, sometimes so violently that it is difficult for those holding the ropes to keep a solid grip. But when the time comes to let go, and the balloon gradually ascends, it becomes completely quiet and still in the basket. The balloon is no longer fighting the wind, it is riding the wind. "Moving with the currents of the wind," my friend told me, "there is no wind. We only feel the wind where there is resistance. When we are *in* the wind, we never *feel* the wind."

Try this: What if we hear *Thy will be done* as *Thy love be done?* What if we feel the *will* of the Creator as the manifest guidance, nourishment, and teaching that springs from the loving heart of our Mother-Father God? Then we may pray *Thy love for me be done. Let thy love for me be realized, let me be receptive to your loving care, wisdom, and guidance.* God's love for us is revealed in the surprising evolution of unpredictable days; our eyes and ears are opened, and we see and hear what we could never have dreamed ourselves. And so we pray simply *Here I am. Thy love for me be done.*

Prayer Practice

"Act as if everything depended on you," counseled Saint Ignatius, "and trust as if everything depended on God."

Thy will be done is a prayer that invites an ever-deepening trust in our dependence on God. As a tool to work with this prayer, I would like to suggest a technique called *centering prayer.* This traditional practice can become a powerful companion in prayer.

Centering prayer is quite simple. First, choose a sacred word or phrase that holds some potent meaning or intention in your life. Then, as you settle into prayerfulness, allow your full attention to rest on your word or phrase. For now, let us choose the phrase *Thy will be done.*

Quietly rest in the phrase; repeat it slowly, let it turn gently in your mind, invite it to find a place in your heart. When attention wanders, gently bring your awareness back to the prayer, *Thy will be done.* Let the words breathe with your breath. Feel their rhythm as they dissolve into your body, becoming part of you. Finally, let yourself rest in silence for a few moments.

You can do centering prayer while sitting quietly with your eyes closed, or you can do it while walking with your eyes open, while on line at the grocery, while driving your car. Whenever you feel unsettled or anxious, allow yourself to surrender your anxiety and bring your attention to this one single thought: *Thy will be done.*

ON EARTH, AS IT IS IN HEAVEN

We enter the household of heaven
when we live fully awake on the earth.

Jesus loved the earth, as did the people who followed him. They were intimately familiar with land and sea, soil and rain. Their lives depended on a fruitful relationship with the natural world. So when Jesus taught about heaven, he used parables from the earth: stories of mustard seeds, how small things grow into large things; stories of seeds that wither when planted in rocky soil but flourish when sown in good soil; how trees are known by their fruits; knowing when the time is ready for harvest; watching how rain falls; and where to find fish in the sea.

We are offered an astonishing, beautiful gift: We can live in heaven right here on the earth. Jesus spoke of lilies of the field and birds of the air, of soil and bread, of seas and vineyards, of nests and wind. Saint Bernard of Clairvaux, a Cistercian monk writing in the twelfth century, echoed Jesus when he confessed that nature was his most reliable spiritual teacher: "What I know of the divine sciences and Holy Scriptures, I learnt in the woods and fields. I have had no other masters than the beeches and the oaks."

Jesus is not giving us instructions to escape this life. Instead, his prayer invites us to sink into that place of deep wholeness where all division between heaven and earth dissolves. The household of heaven is here within us and among us on the earth. He invites us to live simply and kindly on the earth: *Feed the hungry, heal the sick, comfort the lonely, visit the imprisoned, welcome the stranger.* These are simple, practical things, earthly things. Spirituality is not something removed from life on earth. Earth is where heaven lives.

Even in the ecstasy of sexuality—the visceral intercourse of body and spirit—we surrender to a potent river that takes us beyond ourselves, dissolving all boundaries between self and other. God, through our body, offers us spiritual rapture. We are free to taste the sweet blessings we receive through the precious gifts of pleasure in our very human body, a body made of the stuff of the earth, infused with the holy breath of the Spirit.

In this way, the Song of Solomon, a paean to lush

sensuality, is an invitation to spiritual lovemaking, a passionate union of flesh and spirit, sacred intercourse between the human and the divine. "As an apple tree among the trees of the wood, so is my Beloved. . . . Behold, you are beautiful, my love. . . . Your lips are like a scarlet thread. . . . Your two breasts are like two fawns, twins of a gazelle, that feed among the lilies. . . ." This is how heaven is revealed, in sensual communion with the body, in real flesh, real bone.

ON EARTH

At the same time, living in a human body on the earth can be a messy enterprise. Every mother knows that life begins with blood, pain, and tears. As infants, we secrete bodily fluids that seem to soil everything. As children we spill, break, and drop things; as teenagers, we are awash in anguish and uncertainty. As adults we struggle with unexpected and unwanted illnesses, countless injustices, failed relationships, hardships, and infirmities. When we grow old, the body itself deteriorates and finally dies.

This is our inheritance as children of the earth. We are subject to the laws of impermanence and decay. So when we seek refuge in the sanctuary of spiritual practice, it is only natural that our impulse is to pray ourselves into some heaven that is far removed from the sloppy inevitabilities of a life on the earth.

However, while our true nature may be essentially spiritual, we are nonetheless incarnated in human bodies, through which we apprehend joy and sorrow, health and illness, desire and disappointment. Made of dust and spirit, we do not walk the earth as in some foreign place of exile; we are the stuff of which the earth is made. Living on the earth, we are kin to all life. Our bodies are teachers, and our senses—tastes, smells, textures, sounds, images—are doorways through which not only the sorrows but also the gifts of life enter into us.

AS IT IS IN HEAVEN

Thich Nhat Hanh teaches: "The real miracle is not to walk on water or in thin air, but to walk on earth." When we pray *Thy will be done on earth,* we open ourselves to be used as agents of love and healing here and now, for ourselves and for others.

My friend Maryanne left a lucrative massage practice to work with the homeless. For a year she wandered the filthy, urine-soaked sidewalks in the Tenderloin district of San Francisco, offering to massage, with loving care, those who were untouchable. She would ride in the van that picked people up from parks and under bridges when it was cold or raining, massage them in the van, or massage them when they got to the shelter. Her work inspired others to join her, and she now supervises a growing family of interns who offer free massages to the homeless throughout the city.

For the untouchable, God comes in the form of touch. When Maryanne kneads her care into the unwashed shoulders of the poor, her hands feel the sadness, the woundedness, the aches embedded in their weary flesh. When she massages clients in the waiting room at the local health clinic, her "patients" reveal far more to her than they ever do to the doctor about their inner and outer aches and pains, their experience of health and illness. They are always thankful; often there are tears. Some have never received a massage; others have not been touched, with love, in years. For them, this is heaven. For Maryanne, this is prayer.

BREAD FOR THE JOURNEY

Fifteen years ago a group of friends and I started Bread for the Journey, a small organization that seeks out local people who, through their natural generosity, create projects that are simple, caring, and useful. Last year a group of young people in Sebastopol, California, approached us. They were enthusiastically committed to promoting organic gardening, and they offered to volunteer their time, labor, and knowledge to help local people plant organic gardens in their yards.

Bread for the Journey provided seeds and tools to help them get started. The young people asked only two things in return for their work. The first was a donation of a quarter of the seeds from each garden at the end of the season, so that this could become a self-sustaining effort. Second, they required the garden to be planted in people's *front yard*.

This small but subtly ingenious request created a climate of curiosity; people in the neighborhood wanted to see what was being planted, how it was being done. Neighbors, newly engaged, began talking to one another, bringing the community together as they began sharing and working on this new project. It made some neighbors so interested in organic gardening that they asked the young people to help them plant gardens in *their* yards as well. As a result, there are now neighborhoods in Sebastopol where you can walk down the block and see half a dozen front yards blooming with organic flowers and vegetables, neighbors working together, sharing the bounty of their harvest, trading recipes, trading stories of their lives.

Heaven is born on earth in a thousand invisible kindnesses, offered every day. The birth of Jesus revealed that even God begins life on earth as a helpless infant. Heaven, like a newborn baby, needs care, attention, time, and love to grow and thrive. Heaven grows in the soil of small things, a pinch of leaven, a mustard seed, a new garden.

Thy will be done, on earth, as it is in heaven is a call to discover how, through love and kindness, if we are mindful and awake, we can find heaven on earth. The word *temple* shares a root with the word *template,* or model. Our work is to make the earth a model of heaven, where justice flows like a stream, where we live without worry as the lilies of the field, where our body is a temple for the Spirit, where we care for all the children of the earth, the hurt and hungry, the poor and wounded, as if, in Mother Teresa's words, we were caring for Jesus himself "in all his distressing disguises."

Prayer Practice

What if our life on the earth is our prayer? What if we choose one single act—calling someone in need of love, preparing a meal for a friend, visiting someone who aches with loneliness—and imagine that action as our prayer for this day?

We are agents of the divine spirit on the earth. The kindness of God flows through our hands, our words, our work, our actions. Today, pray with your hands. Not by clasping your hands in a holy gesture, but by using them to bring some good and necessary gift to someone in need.

We can also use these small tasks as an opportunity to expand our practice of centering prayer. At every moment, while eating, speaking, or performing the smallest daily task, we can focus our prayer on this phrase: *Thy will be done, on earth, as it is in heaven.*

GIVE US THIS DAY
OUR DAILY BREAD

Everything we need for this day
is given to us lovingly and freely.

Here, at the center of the prayer, we subtly shift our awareness to the desires of our heart. We have settled into prayer, honoring the luminous aspects of the Divine: the household of heaven, thy name, thy kingdom, thy will. Now we turn our attention to those needs and yearnings that have been growing within us, beneath language, waiting to be spoken. And the first thing we ask is to receive nourishment. Most notably, we ask for bread, for this one single day.

What is our daily bread? At first we think of food, the most basic of our physical needs. When the people of Israel wandered the desert in exile, they were hungry. In response to their cries for food, God fed them with manna from heaven, bread that "was like coriander seed, white, and the taste of it was like wafers made

85

with honey." Aside from its sweetness, the other distinctive quality of manna was that it would not keep overnight. God, through Moses, told the Israelites to "gather of it, each one of you, as much as you can eat." However, if anyone took more than they needed for that day and hoarded a secret reserve, by the next morning it would breed worms and become foul. This was a lesson in trust, in faith, to remind them again and again that God would give them each day what they needed. To hoard more than their daily bread would be to mistrust God's unfailing kindness and grace.

Similarly, after the Buddha died, his students and followers gathered to consider the precepts by which they would live and practice. One of their first principles concerned food: Monks were not allowed to keep food overnight. Each morning they had to beg for their daily bread. Making the rounds of the village with their begging bowl, they relied on the basic premise that whatever they were given that day would be, for them, enough.

The day is the canvas on which we paint our life, the container in which we practice our good and necessary work. *This is the day the Lord has made, let us rejoice and be glad in it.* The day is the garden in which we plant our seeds; nothing grows anywhere but in the soil of this one single day. Having worked for many years with alcoholics and addicts who find courage and healing in twelve-step programs, I know that the prescription to live "one day at a time" is not just a clever aphorism; it is a lifesaving decision.

WHAT IS ENOUGH?

Give us this day our daily bread. What is, for us, daily bread? How do we precisely assess our simplest requirements for a life well lived? How do we honestly determine what is, for us, this day, *enough*?

Each day we respond anew to this challenge. In our fear, or in the hectic desperation of our accelerating lives, we often overestimate our genuine needs. We do not take time to carefully discern our authentic requirements. Instead, we are seduced by the swirling desires of the mind, the rampant seductions of the marketplace, always demanding more and more, hoping that somehow, in the sheer volume of what we acquire, we will find fulfillment or joy.

But often we simply end up with a mess. We hoard mounds of unnecessary possessions and responsibilities, wondering what to do with them all. How much simpler our life would be if we had only to care for this day, to be concerned with this day's food, this day's responsibility, this day's prayer. *Do not be anxious about tomorrow*, said Jesus, *let tomorrow be anxious about itself.*

When we pray for our daily bread, we pray for more than food: *We do not live by bread alone,* Jesus would say. We thirst for more than mere survival. Even prisoners in concentration camps were given food, yet it is cruel to presume they were truly fed. If we are lonely, only the loving company of another can become our daily bread. If we are sad, we hunger for beauty, hope, and delight. If we feel scattered and overwhelmed, we may require the bread of quiet solitude, or contemplative prayer. If we are weary, we need sweet repose; if we are frightened, we seek reassurance and comfort; if we are joyful, we look to share our bread with others. Each of these simple human needs is kneaded into the bread of *enough.*

Our search for "spiritual abundance," so common in contemporary spiritual conversation, is subtly motivated by a lingering presumption of scarcity. If we are afraid there is not enough for us, we will grab for abundance, which is actually *more* than we need. Thus, even in abundance, there is great fear.

There is a crucial difference between *abundance*—a fearful response to scarcity—and *sufficiency*—which invites the possibility of genuine satisfaction and well-being. Sufficiency is that moment when we have enough. After a meal, our craving for food dissolves. After we have arrived at our destination, we no longer need the map that brought us there. After a drink from a cool fountain, we are no longer desperate to find water. The instant we have enough, dissatisfaction and desire melt away.

When we are attentive and awake, a single breath can fill us to overflowing. The touch of a loved one, a particular angle of sunlight can bring delight to our hearts. The simple gesture of someone's hand resting in our own, a taste of honey, or a strain of melody can, each in their own way, become our daily bread.

BREAD FOR THE WORLD

At the same time, we must never lose sight of the fact that the need for bread in the world is painfully real. *Thirty-five thousand children die every single day from hunger and hunger-related illnesses.* For these children, daily bread is no spiritual metaphor. God comes to the hungry in the form of real food. This is why we pray, not for *my* daily bread, but for *our* daily bread. We are praying not only for our own sustenance, but also for the wisdom, courage, and strength on this day to offer what we can to help nourish the world and provide food for all the children of the earth.

Just as waves gradually grind rock into sand, this prayer wears away our individual needs so that we may feel ourselves part of something infinitely larger, and meditate on our place in an enormous family that stands in great need of nourishment. When we take more than we need, it is less likely that those who are truly hungry will receive their share. So our prayer for *our daily bread* challenges us to be part of the healing of the world, to imagine that part of *our* daily bread is insuring that those who are hungry receive *their* daily bread.

GIVE US THIS DAY
OUR DAILY REST

Daily bread refers not only to *having* enough, but also to *doing* enough. In the world of relentless striving and accomplishment, we rarely feel we have done enough to earn our daily bread. This corrosive feeling—that we always have so much more to do—makes us bone-weary.

This pervasive belief—that if we just work harder, longer, and faster, we will "get it all done"—is our model of a successful career. If we work and work and work, then, when we have finally fulfilled some impossible expectation of what is enough, we earn our right to rest, to retire, to enjoy the fruits of our labor.

When I first began my work as a parish minister I met Tom, a kind, delightful man who had worked for a tractor-manufacturing company for thirty years. After decades of travel, overtime, and dedication to the company, he finally saved enough to retire. Together he and his wife, Marcella, moved from the Midwest to Santa Fe and built a beautiful home, large enough to accommodate visiting children, grandchildren, and guests. Tom began slowing down as he eased into a retirement he hoped would give him back all the precious time he had traded away, time now to be with his children, time to volunteer at church, time to play golf.

One morning I was called to the hospital. I found myself standing with Marcella as the doctors told her that Tom had inoperable pancreatic cancer. Within two weeks, as Marcella and I sat together with him in his hospital room, Tom—on a morphine drip to numb the horrible pain—stopped breathing. We sat together in the silence, aware of the sudden absence of breath. Tom had passed away, quietly, in his sleep. He finally had his retirement.

If we wait too long, we will never taste what we have already been given. When we pray, we ask for the wisdom to know what is for us, this day, enough. *Oh, gracious Mother, Spirit God who lives in the mustard seed, who offers us heaven on earth, teach us to feel the shape of enough in this day.* Prayer is a revolutionary practice that challenges us to dissolve our habitual cravings and instead become mindful of our simplest needs, slowly tracing the outline of what is for us, this day, sufficient daily bread.

When we mindfully receive our daily bread, our days naturally give way to gratitude and thanksgiving. Meister Eckhart, the Christian mystic, said that if the only prayer you ever say in your whole life is *Thank you,* that would be enough. This is a twofold prayer: We ask for the bread we need, and we give thanks for the bread we have.

Benjamin Hunch, a Navajo boy, writes about his grandmother, a living picture of a woman nourished by her daily bread:

> *The old lady is sitting*
> *outside the hogan*
> *weaving a rug,*
> *with her white hair*
> *going back and forth in the air as the wind*
> *goes by very slow,*
> *her fingers moving like the legs of a spider,*
> *with her mind full*
> *of the things that she*
> *did before she got old,*
> *and her mind on the rug,*
> *forgetting all about*
> *the things she had planned*
> *to do for the day, and her*
> *eyes just moving upon the wind.*

At times, this is all we need: something beautiful to hold in our hand, a sweet memory, and eyes that can follow the wind. In this moment, nothing more is required. For now, we can forget whatever else we thought we needed to have or to do, and rest in the fullness of this moment. For now, this is enough. This is heaven. This is our daily bread.

Prayer Practice

In morning prayer, meditate on this question: *What do I imagine would be enough for me today?* Then, in evening prayer, ask yet another question: *Can I make peace with whatever I have been given—all the joys and sorrows, the gifts and challenges, the surprises and disappointments—and honestly give thanks for all of it?* As we end the day, we say simply, *Thank you for everything.*

FORGIVE US
OUR TRESPASSES

*When we acknowledge and confess
our errors and mistakes, to ourselves and
to God, deep, genuine healing begins.*

Why do we pray? One thing seems constant and true: When we pray, we ask that our heart may be cleansed and clear, freed of turmoil and anguish, so we may rest in a state of wholeness and peace.

What hampers this state of heaven, and how can we find peace when we feel so terribly lost? Few things erode our serenity more reliably than the corrosive memory of any harm we may have done to others. If we are ashamed of something we have done, we will lie about who we are. Our shame imprisons and isolates us from those who would offer us their love—our family, colleagues, and closest friends. With each successive secret we become smaller, more boxed in, shut in by the walls of our fear of being discovered.

Sadly, many of us believe we must be perfect and

without blemish in order to be deserving of God's love. We are ashamed of our imperfections, and we try to hide our shortcomings. This fearful secrecy gradually erodes any peace or serenity we may hope for. When we pray to be forgiven, we are really praying to be set free from this toxic prison of shame, hiding, and pretense. We are praying to be accepted—even loved—for all that we are.

When Jesus uses the phrase *Forgive us our trespasses,* he presumes we will trespass upon the lives of others. How many of us can say we have never brought harm to another, intentionally or unintentionally? It is absurd even to consider. As human beings, we make mistakes. This is what we do. In our daily pilgrimage of making a living, advancing our career, interacting with friends and colleagues, living with lovers and families and spouses and children, we make mistakes.

We get angry, we get frustrated, we say an unkind thing, we tell a small but hurtful lie, we take something that does not really belong to us, we quietly take advantage of someone else for our own personal gain. We do this because we are human, we are fallible, and we are imperfect. Perhaps this is the distinguishing mark of our humanity: our inexhaustible capacity for imperfection.

THE HEALING POWER
OF CONFESSION

So when we pray *Forgive us our trespasses,* we are preparing ourselves to confess, honestly and openly, our essential humanity. An ancient definition of the word *confess* is "to declare or reveal one's identity." To confess is to share one's whole self, to declare both good and bad, what is seen in public and what is hidden in private. Not so that we may be punished, but rather so we may cleanse our hearts, set free what has been shamefully imprisoned, throw open the windows and allow in fresh air and light.

Prayer, then, is an exquisite opportunity to cease pretending to be other than we are, to relinquish the exhausting habit of keeping up appearances. We are free to speak plainly about our shortcomings, let go of our defenses, drop the big show we put on for the world, let down our guard and tell the truth. Only when we honestly confess the whole truth of who we are can we receive honest love in return. Otherwise, we can never feel truly and completely seen and loved. Concealing our secret inner life prevents us from drinking deep from the healing grace and unconditional forgiveness of God.

Sometimes, at the end of a long and frustrating day, I

may be impatient or curt with my twelve-year-old son, Max. If—when I realize I have been unkind—I do not apologize, if out of shame or denial I do not acknowledge that I have acted badly, then my actions pollute the air of our family life. Perhaps Max will begin to believe I do not care for him as much as I do. Perhaps I will keep trying to shield him from my imperfections so as to seem infallible. But then he will mistrust me, or he will begin to mistrust his own feelings and perceptions. He will withdraw a little, in imperceptible ways, and we will both lose the sweet nourishment of each other's company.

But if I say to my son, "I am sorry I yelled. I was tired, I was upset that you were not listening, but know that I love you with all my heart, now and always, even when I am upset with you." Then we are clean, there is no residue to poison our time together, and in a few moments we can be playing and laughing together. The truth has set us free.

It is our deep and unshakable love for each other that allows me to be honest about my shortcomings. I know that at the end of the day Max and I will still love each other. God's love for us is just like mine for my son: It is unconditional. We can only ask forgiveness if we know in the cells of our bones that we will, in spite of everything, always remain beloved children of our Creator.

LIBERATING OURSELVES
WHILE MAKING AMENDS

I have spent many years among alcoholics and addicts who diligently work to heal the deep anguish of their disease through some program of recovery, often based on the twelve steps of Alcoholics Anonymous. The majority of those steps presume that our deepest healing rests in our capacity to address unacknowledged shortcomings in ourselves. Indeed, seven of the twelve steps specifically target our willingness to recognize, admit, and correct the myriad ways we are destructive to ourselves and to others:

Made a searching and fearless moral inventory of
　　ourselves;
Admitted to God, to ourselves, and to another
　　human being the exact nature of our wrongs;
Were entirely ready to have God remove all
　　those defects of character;

Humbly asked him to remove our shortcomings;

Made a list of all persons we had harmed, and became willing to make amends to them all;

Made direct amends to such people wherever possible, except when to do so would injure them or others;

Continued to take personal inventory, and when we were wrong, promptly admitted it.

These seven steps, taken together, could reasonably be condensed into a single phrase: *Forgive us our trespasses.* If we are to heal the world, we must begin with ourselves.

Jesus said, *Judge not, that ye be not judged.* When seeking to heal the suffering and hatred in the world, he insisted we begin by taking inventory of our own offenses: *First take the log out of your own eye, that you may see more clearly the splinter in your brother's or sister's eye.*

When the abhorrent policy of apartheid was abolished in South Africa, Archbishop Desmond Tutu and others created the Truth and Reconciliation Commission, guided by the African concept of *ubuntu*—that *people are people through other people.*

In practical terms, this meant that in order to heal the deep gash that had bloodied their land, people on all sides of the conflict—soldiers, government officials, townspeople, prisoners, families of murdered sons and daughters, mothers and fathers—were called to come forward and publicly confess their stories. Murderers faced families of their victims, poor blacks faced white soldiers who had raped and tortured them. Only with the sacramental communion of truth-telling could the lingering residue of hatred begin to dissipate, making room for an entire nation to walk a path toward healing.

In his final report, Archbishop Tutu summarized the work of the commission in this way:

Having looked the beast of the past in the eye, having asked and received forgiveness and having made amends, let us shut the door on the past—not in order to forget it but in order not to allow it to imprison us. Let us move into the glorious future of a new kind of society where people count, not because of biological irrelevancies or other extraneous attributes, but because they are persons of infinite worth created in the image of God. . . .

TELLING THE TRUTH

Early in my career I worked with a young alcoholic named Jenny. Jenny began drinking when she was twelve, and was sent to me by the court when she was twenty-two. Already her body seemed old, sick, and weary. She had been arrested more than once, mangled countless friendships, squandered a string of jobs, and now felt desperate, angry, and alone. Her addiction caused her untold pain and suffering beyond her years, and finally brought her into treatment.

Along the way Jenny also caused a great deal of sorrow for others. She lied relentlessly to her friends, betrayed the trust of those who tried to help her, and abused the love of her family. Her mother, Ruth, drawing on a deep pool of maternal love, was the one person who tried to stay close to Jenny, even as she broke promise after promise to get help; even as Jenny came home, sweet and sober, only to steal money and disappear for weeks; even as Jenny, in the middle of the night, called to cry, to scream, to berate her mother for not helping her enough.

Now, finally in therapy, the time had come for Jenny to speak the truth, to confess honestly the ways in which she, in her addiction, brought her mother so much anguish and sorrow. In my office, they faced each other. Jenny was silent for what felt like a very long time. "I know that I hurt you," Jenny began slowly, measuring her words. "I now understand that I am an alcoholic, and because of that I did some bad things. Some of them I don't even remember." Jenny searched her mother's face for some sign of how she would respond. Ruth was silent and unmoved. Jenny, hesitant, reluctant, continued.

"I guess I did some things I shouldn't have, but it was because of my disease. I know that now. I did a lot of stupid things, but that's over. From now on, things will be better." Again, Jenny waited. But Ruth had heard much of this before. Promises, excuses, half-baked apologies. She wasn't hearing anything she hadn't already heard a hundred times from Jenny. She exhaled, her head fell a little, disclosing a weariness from someplace very deep, very old.

Perhaps Jenny saw her mother's weariness; perhaps she had seen it before and run from it, but in this moment she truly saw her mother's pain. She saw the years of care and worry, all the times Ruth stayed close when others fled, felt her mother's everlasting, unconditional love for her, a love Jenny had so carelessly abused in her confusion, her hurt, her despair.

Something in Jenny shifted, and when she spoke, her voice was tender, honest, like a little girl's. "I am sorry, Mama," Jenny said quietly, looking directly at her mother's face. "I am so sorry." She began to weep. "I am so sorry. I never wanted to hurt you."

Those few simple words liberated something that, in time, would begin to heal years of hurt that had passed between them. Ruth reached out for her daughter, and Jenny collapsed in her arms, repeating, "I am so sorry, I am so sorry," like a prayer, over and over, her mother quietly whispering, "It's all right, it's all right," and they both wept for a very long time.

BLESSING OUR MISTAKES

When Catholics enter the confessional they begin by saying, "Bless me, for I have sinned." Not "judge me, punish me, berate me," but "bless me." A sin, then, is an invitation to bless and be blessed.

What does this mean, to sin? Jesus insisted we are all sinners. Is he saying we are all bad people? This is impossible. The word we translate as *sin* is, in the original Greek of the Gospels, *hamartia*. *Hamartia* is a word ancient Greeks used in the sporting events that became the model for our contemporary Olympics. In archery, a target was set up, and a line of competitors were arranged a certain distance away. Archers took their respective turns, while a judge monitored the target. If an archer missed the mark, the judge would call out, *"Hamartia!"*

To sin, then, is to miss the mark. To be off center. To act in such a way that, whatever our skill or intention, we fall short. This is the original meaning of sin.

Every day, in a hundred ways, we all miss the mark. Some of us harbor terribly unrealistic expectations, believing that a life well lived is one in which, after years of diligent prayer, worship, and practice, we finally learn to live without ever missing the mark. But we are human, and missing the mark is simply what we do. The more useful question is this: Having missed the mark, again and again, in spite of our prayers and intentions, what do we do now?

The answer is clear. If your sin brings harm to yourself, forgive yourself. If your sin brings harm to another, ask their forgiveness. When we are ensnared in a prison of our own shame and regret, only confession and forgiveness can set us free to enter the household of heaven.

What does this mean, to ask forgiveness? It means

we speak the truth. We name what has happened. We acknowledge that harm was done, and that we had some part in it, intentionally or unintentionally. Some of the most dramatic scandals of our day were driven less by the gravity of the sin than by the attempt to cover it up. If we cause harm, it is our prayer to be clear and honest enough to plainly admit our complicity in something that brought injury to the world.

LEARNING FROM OUR MISTAKES

When we confess our trespasses in prayer, we can begin to hear the teaching embedded in each mistake. Our lives are shaped as by water on stone; teachings arrive without ceasing in the reverberations of our repeated errors. We make the same mistakes again and again, until one day we hear their message; there is a better path, a truer way to live. When we finally receive the teaching, the need to repeat the same mistakes gradually falls away.

Our sins are not our judges, they are our teachers. Confessing them allows us to set a more accurate and loving course for our life. Awake to the effects of our words and deeds, we can recalibrate our inner compass, and begin again. This is the literal meaning of the word *repent*: to turn around, to set off in a new direction, to begin again.

Every action ripples into the world. Everything we do and say has consequences. We are inexorably and intimately woven into the web of our friends, our family, our colleagues, the entire family of the earth. If we cause harm and do not repair it, the seeds of that harm will grow in untold and unexpected ways.

But if we confess our trespasses and ask forgiveness, we become willing to be taken, to be swept clean, to be ready for the healing balm of heaven.

Prayer Practice

As you settle into quietude, allow your heart to be drawn into the territory of something difficult or unfinished. Feel the memory of having, intentionally or unintentionally, brought harm to another.

Feel how the body tightens around the heart, how you hold or defend, how you constrict or withdraw. This is the subtle prison of the unconfessed secret.

Call up the image of the Spirit you invoke in prayer,

and allow the loving Creator to enfold you in safety. Then, choose one small act that remains with you, a painful memory of harm done to another. Speak aloud the honest confession of your error or mistake; speak the truth, feel where it still lives in memory, in the tissue of your body. Be aware of what happens when the container that has held it for so long begins to melt.

As an expansion of your prayer, you may wish to make amends, if it is possible and useful, to the one you hurt. It need not be something dramatic; a simple apology, an honest conversation, or a word of regret may be sufficient. Again, be aware of any shift in weight or pressure in your heart when you have finally allowed what was hidden to be spoken aloud, lifted up, and acknowledged to be true.

AS WE FORGIVE THOSE WHO TRESPASS AGAINST US

When we offer forgiveness to others,
it becomes a powerful sacrament
that sets us free.

I was leading a retreat with a group of people who had come seeking sustenance and refuge from their busy lives. We spent time in tender conversation, listening for those inner voices that are audible only in a circle of trust and sanctuary. As often happens, we began to hear of places and times when some had been hurt or abused in their lives. We could feel in one another where the gash of woundedness ran deep and the persistence of memory seared the body, mind, and heart.

Katharine was a strong, creative woman who, as a child, had been deeply scarred by a mother who had been relentlessly critical and overbearing. She shared with the group that, as a child, in her mother's eyes, Katharine could do nothing right. Her mother bombarded her with a constant flow of insults and accusations about her incompetence and stupidity. For much of her adult life Katharine struggled to find her own strength and peace, but even as she grew older she remained haunted by lingering, festering resentments about her mother's cruelty.

At a retreat we normally devote time for prayer, and at one point we were about to pray together the Lord's Prayer. I was mindful of how Katharine had confessed her anger toward her mother. I knew she yearned to be free from the anguish of wrestling with these resentments. Nevertheless, there was a part of Katharine that was not at all ready to forgive her mother. And so I playfully invited Katharine to explore her willingness to let go of her mother's unkindness. When we prayed together, I suggested we would say, "Forgive us our trespasses, as we forgive those who trespass against us"—and then all add aloud, in unison, "EXCEPT KATHARINE'S MOTHER!"

A ripple of laughter passed through the room, as we each recalled someone in our own lives—a parent, an employer, a neighbor, an enemy, a friend—whom we were particularly reluctant to forgive. So as we prayed, when we all shouted together, "EXCEPT KATHARINE'S MOTHER!" Katharine smiled. She was delighted by this playful camaraderie, and humbled by her connection to so many who were, like herself, caught in the confusing web of hurt and forgiveness.

Years later, Katharine told me that retreat was a turning point for her. "That prayer was the beginning of a deeper healing with my mother," she said. "I saw how silly it all was, how much I was holding on. On that day it dawned on me I might finally be able to let go, that my attachment to my mother's cruelty could finally begin to dissolve."

THE REQUIREMENT TO FORGIVE

In the entirety of the Lord's Prayer, the only act specifically required of us is *the act of forgiveness*. The rest—*thy kingdom come, thy will be done, give us our daily bread, forgive us our trespasses, deliver us from evil*—are all petitions for clarity, nourishment, and safety. In the midst of these petitions we are called to perform only one singular act: to forgive those who bring us harm.

Jesus spends a great deal of time instructing his disciples on the indispensability of forgiveness on the path to spiritual freedom. *In prayer,* he says, *there is a connection*

between what God does and what you do. You can't get for-
giveness from God without also forgiving others. If you refuse
to do your part, you cut yourself off from God's part.

Expanding his teaching further, he insists we should
not even approach the altar of prayer or communion
without first resolving any hurt or conflict with another. *First be reconciled to your brother and sister, and then*
come and offer your gift, he said. According to Jesus, our
unwillingness to forgive tarnishes our capacity to receive the nourishment and liberation we seek in prayer.

Most of us hold tightly to the recollection of all the
ways we have been hurt. Closing our fist around how
this or that person hurt or dishonored us, we are
trapped in a dance of suffering with that person forever.
We revisit their abuse every time that person enters our
thoughts.

Again and again we relive the suffering, calling it up
over and over, as if sheer repetition could somehow
erase the tape. But each repetition deepens the rut of
anguish that corrodes our peace. When we hold our
abusers hostage, the recollected hurt simultaneously
holds us hostage. We are forever locked in an inner
prison of our own making. If we want to be free, we
must choose to leave our self-imposed exile in the past,
and move boldly into forgiveness.

RESISTING FORGIVENESS

How can we do this? Without forgiveness, genuine spiritual freedom is impossible. And yet what is more difficult, more excruciating, than offering the precious gift of forgiveness to someone who has hurt us deeply, abused us, broken our heart?

I have been privileged to be close to many who harbor seemingly unbearable wounds. Jim was betrayed by his wife, who left him and their children to live with her secret lover. Maria was raped repeatedly as a child by her father. Barbara was beaten so badly by her husband that she finally took refuge in a shelter, where her broken bones could heal. Janice was fired by her boss for refusing his sexual advances, and she had to seek welfare to support her children. Robert and Susan lost both their children in an automobile accident, killed by a drunken driver. Still, in the midst of our agony and distress, we are called to forgive the ones who took so much, who ruined our lives. This is not an easy pill to swallow.

The reasons to hate are legion. The thirst for retribution, to extract an eye for an eye and a tooth for a tooth, seems right, balanced, and just. Indeed, prayer for forgiveness does not exclude justice. We are called to work tirelessly to insure that those who do cause violence, oppression, and abuse are brought to justice, so we may cultivate a fertile, honest peace, to bring this peace of heaven to earth.

But the simple physics of retribution demonstrate that, in the long run, our natural urge to answer hurt for hurt inevitably perpetuates an endless cycle of violence and hatred in which we are trapped forever. How can we free our hearts to enter the household of heaven, even though we have been hurt, betrayed, or mistreated by the world?

CULTIVATING A READINESS TO FORGIVE

While forgiveness may be the singular act that will ultimately set us free, our capacity to forgive grows slowly. In prayer, we pray for this readiness, some deep willingness or capacity to forgive those who have harmed us so terribly. But even as we pray for this healing, it can only be invited and nurtured, never rushed or pushed. It has its own timing. As the sea wears down the rocky shore, the invitation to forgive takes time to dilute the ever-fresh sting of remembered injustice. When we pray, we pray for this season of forgiveness to come.

The ancient Greek language has two distinct words for time. The first, *chronos,* describes chronological time, the measure of successive minutes, hours, and years. The second, *kairos,* is the word Jesus used when he said, "The time is fulfilled." *Kairos* is the fullness of time, the readiness of things to be born and to blossom in their own ripe unfolding.

So it is with forgiveness. When we enter into the practice of prayer, we pray to be made ready. We pray to prepare our hearts to soften and open, in time, as the snows of winter slowly melt, gradually bringing life-giving water to the parched places where new life waits to grow.

My friend Dick Nethercutt was a parishioner at the church in Massachusetts where I first apprenticed as a minister. Dick and his wife, Lorraine, adopted a baby girl, Jaina, who grew to be a strong-willed teenager, and later an adventurous young woman who left home to attend the University of Washington. One day Jaina and her boyfriend decided to visit Seattle, where they spent the night at an inexpensive hotel. That night they were both murdered in their room. Jaina was raped, and then strangled with a pair of nylon stockings. A thirty-five-year-old man was later convicted of her murder.

Two years later, Dick continued to struggle to find some meaning, some healing, in the tragedy that had befallen his daughter. He felt a strong need to contact her killer, to make sense, to find redemption.

At the advice of a priest, Dick finally, reluctantly, made contact with the prison in Washington. After many long and painful discussions with the prison chaplain there, it was arranged that his daughter's killer would call Dick on the phone. "I was stunned. I couldn't possibly know what to say. I mumbled and fumbled some words to him. I was surprised that I didn't feel any anger; he was already being punished for what he had done. Somehow, at the end of our conversation, the words 'I forgive you' came out of my mouth. But I certainly did not feel it in my heart at the time. Real forgiveness took a good deal longer."

Dick began visiting inmates at the correctional institution near his home. He needed to piece together the broken pieces of his life, and try to create something good and positive out of the horror of his daughter's murder. He started an Alternatives to Violence program, speaking with inmates about his loss, and about the terrible costs of violence to everyone, victim and perpetrator alike. "The inmates offered me great sympathy for my loss, and I realized I could offer a gift by sharing what happened to Jaina. I saw how we were each imprisoning ourselves, unless we were all willing to let go of our own feelings of anger and hate."

Twenty years after Jaina's death, Dick shared with me how long his journey toward forgiveness had been. "Forgiveness doesn't mean forgetting. I will never forget what happened to my daughter. Forgiveness means forgiving the individual, not forgiving or condoning the horrible crime. Forgiveness lets me move on, move forward. It has been a powerful and freeing experience for me."

PRAYER AND SPACIOUSNESS

There is a Tibetan parable about water and salt. First, take a tablespoon of salt and stir it until it dissolves in a cup of water. If you drink the water in the cup it will leave a terrible taste in the mouth. But if you take that very same tablespoon of salt and dissolve it in an enormous, clear, blue mountain lake, and then drink the water from the lake, the water still tastes sweet.

The problem, the Tibetans say, is not the salt. The problem is the size of the container that holds the salt. If the container is ample and deep, our primary experience, even as the salt dissolves, our primary experience will be the taste of clear, fresh water.

Forgiveness requires a deep willingness to become more spacious. When we pray to be able to forgive, we are praying to be made larger, to become so ample and clearheaded that we can bear even this hurt, this abuse, this loss, while still feeling blessed by the deep and faithful company of God. The salt in the wound is painful indeed; but if we pray, and pray, and pray, over time—in its time—our heart may open and become as tranquil as clear water in a mountain lake.

Without forgiveness, our lives can never change. Look to the Middle East, to the Balkans, to urban gangs, to our own troubled families, anywhere there is no lasting forgiveness. The searing ache of memory without forgiveness gives birth again and again to an astonishingly faithful duplication of the sufferings of the past in the present moment.

FORGIVING GOD

As we forgive the ones who brought us suffering, we must also forgive the fact that there is suffering at all. Why, we ask, does God allow suffering to infect the fabric of creation? Must we forgive even God?

My friend Preston and his son Leander decided to take a camping trip together. It was Leander's thirteenth birthday, and they wanted to celebrate his passage into young adulthood.

They drove into the mountains of Colorado, where they camped, hiked, talked, and dreamed about what their futures might bring. When the time came to leave, it turned out to be an exquisite day of sun and blue sky, crisp air and limitless views. Preston wanted to get home before dark, but agreed to take one final hike before they left.

They began to climb, and after an hour Preston told Leander they needed to turn back. Leander insisted they climb to the summit, and Preston found it impossible to object. Such moments are rare in the lives of fathers and sons. When they reached the summit, Leander was thrilled; it was the first peak he had ever climbed.

Finally, Preston led the way down the mountain. At

a certain point he turned around to check on Leander. At that moment, he heard what he thought was a rockslide. He backtracked, only to see that his son had fallen off the trail onto the rocks below. His body was not moving.

Preston rushed down and held his son. In a few moments, his breathing stopped. Leander died in his father's arms. Preston, stunned and confused, lifted his son's body on his back. With Leander's head limp on his shoulder, he carried him out of the wilderness.

For a long time Preston wrestled with his grief and his anger. He was angry at the mountain, angry with himself, angry with God. "I went into hell," Preston told me. "I felt animal-like pain, my heart was ripped open. I screamed at God, an agonizing grief. Why did this happen? Why did I let him climb that mountain? Why did God take him now?"

Two years later, Preston returned to the mountain, in search of healing, a kind of peace. He climbed the summit, he wept, he yelled at God. "I heard a voice say, *Let me have it! I am the universal force—tell me everything.* It was not the voice of some faraway, distant God; it seemed a comforting presence. I said everything I'd ever needed to say. Slowly, I began to feel the tender beginnings of forgiveness. I realized I had to forgive myself for taking Leander on the trip, for letting him climb the mountain, for not being able to save him. I had been punishing myself ever since.

"I had to make peace with my human fallibility. I had done everything I could do. As I forgave myself, forgiving God came easily. In the act of forgiveness, I could take the event and allow it to be transformed into a blessing. I was grateful for the gift of my son, for our time together, the love we shared. I am much more mindful of how precious is the love that moves between people. I discovered prayer in the core of my heart. Before, God always felt far away. Now, God feels close, and strong. I am unbelievably thankful for the life of my son."

To forgive is to bear what we are given; to acknowledge that we have been afflicted with pain, loss, or harm, but then to bless it all, and let it be. We pray, in this moment, to take refuge in God, to dissolve into the enormity of heaven, comforted by the healing spirit of the world. Only then, when we have become so much larger than our sorrows, may we stride confidently in the direction of our dreams, allowing the mistakes of the past to dissolve and fall away, leaving us free and ready to partake, awake and alive, of the sweet harvest of our daily bread.

Prayer Practice

Allow the image of someone who has harmed you to arise in your mind. You may even wish to look at a photograph of them. As you prepare your heart to forgive, be patient and gentle with yourself. Allow the words to come slowly; acknowledge any resistance as a natural, human reluctance to forgive. If you can, touch even this resistance with mercy and kindness.

Say aloud, *For all that you have done that caused me pain, intentionally or unintentionally, through your actions or your words, I forgive you. I forgive you. I set you free. I set myself free from you, and from the harm you did to me.*

Notice the resistance; sense when the heart tries to harden and hold the anger, fear, or hatred. When resistance arises, turn your awareness to the gentle rhythm of your breath, and use the centering phrase *I forgive you, I set us both free* to recalibrate your deep intention to forgive. Then begin again: *I forgive you. I forgive you.* Let the heart soften. Let the war be over. Set them free. Set yourself free. *I set you free. I am free from you. I set us free. God bless you. Go in peace.*

Take as much time as you need to sense any genuine freedom and relief. It may take many sessions to feel complete; repeat this practice until you notice some sense of closure or liberation. Forgiveness takes time, courage, and compassion. There is no need to rush or hurry. It is simply an invitation to be set free, to walk unencumbered into the household of heaven.

LEAD US NOT INTO TEMPTATION

*Our temptations are our greatest teachers;
they clearly mirror the unresolved
confusions of the heart and
soul, and allow us to heal them.*

For some of us, *Lead us not into temptation* can be a confusing prayer. Do we actually believe God willfully leads us into potential danger and temptation? Why would a supposedly loving God be so manipulative, continually testing our loyalty and our faith?

It is a good and fair question. How can we pray *Lead us not into temptation* and not fear that our Creator is acting like a Machiavellian puppeteer, setting us up, waiting to see if we will be knocked down by temptations greater than our character can withstand?

Perhaps we must listen more deeply: What exactly is temptation? How does it work, and what spiritual function does it provide? After Jesus was baptized by John in the Jordan, he was immediately required to undertake a spiritual quest. He was called out into the wilderness to pray. There, for forty days and forty nights, he fasted, he prayed, and, when he was physically weak—yet spiritually clear—he was tempted by Satan.

Satan is a figure who symbolizes the satisfaction of all desires, the purveyor of all the glittery baubles that attract the endless cravings of the mind. Satan plays on our desires, promising satisfaction of all our cravings, if only we will abandon the ways of the Spirit and surrender to the ways of material gain.

But if we look closely, we discover that unbridled desire often leads to greater sorrow. Indeed, the Buddha taught that our endless craving and thirst is in fact the source of suffering. Desire is our yearning for what we do not possess, producing dissatisfaction with what we have, an aversion to our current life, so that we continually want life to be different, rather than accepting things as they are. Desire is the opposite of serenity and acceptance; it stands in stark opposition to the practice of *Thy will be done.*

When Satan appears to Jesus, he first tempts Jesus to turn stones to bread—in part to feed himself, and in part to prove his spiritual power. At this point, Jesus is hungry, thirsty, alone, perhaps even frightened. Who among us is so strong, so certain of our calling, our identity, and our character, that we would not, in that moment, trade almost anything for water and bread?

But Jesus refuses, saying, *Man does not live by bread alone, but by every word that proceeds from the mouth of God.*

Next, Satan suggests Jesus throw himself off a high place. If Jesus is truly beloved of God, surely the angels of heaven would come to his aid, lift him up and protect him. Again, Jesus refuses to flaunt his spiritual importance. Finally, Satan offers him the biggest prize of all—dominion over all the kingdoms of the world—in exchange for Jesus' allegiance only to him. Jesus refuses one last time to trade his devotion to God for fame, power, or influence in the world.

After forty days of solitary exile, Jesus is offered everything a hungry, tired, lonely person could ever want: food, honor, and power. To all three temptations Jesus said: No, no, no. I know who I am. My life is not about what I can do, or about how important I am, or about how much power or influence I can have. I am loved by God. If I dedicate my life to power and illusion—rather than love and service to God—I walk right into a prison that would choke and diminish my soul. The instant he rejects these temptations, the angels of heaven come and care for him, comfort him, and minister to him.

When Jesus resists the temptations of desire, he recognizes and claims his strength and affirms his identity. In the end, he can only be certain of the reliable depth and breadth of his true nature if that essential nature is tested in some way.

WHY TEMPTATION?

To be tested is not a bad thing. Temptation calls us out of the comfort of our ordinary lives in order to learn something extraordinary about ourselves.

The Hebrews were tested in the desert for forty years before they could enter the Promised Land as the people of God. Job, nearly crushed by unbearable misfortune, illness, and loss, was tempted to curse the God who made him. Nevertheless, he reached far into some unimaginable place of faith, and rededicated his spiritual allegiance to his Creator.

When the Buddha sat down under the cover of the Bodhi tree, he resolved to remain there until he discovered the deepest truths about himself and the world. As he moved ever closer to these truths, he was beset by demons who sought to seduce him from his task, to lure him away from his vow, to destroy his resolve. Only after he defeated these temptations did he finally, at the rising of the morning star, fully realize the beauty and perfection of his true nature.

Because these stories are old and familiar, it is easy to dismiss them as fables and myths. After all, the deck is stacked, and in these stories good always wins out over evil, and the holy seekers always triumph in the end.

But what if we hear them differently? Jesus, Job, and the Buddha, tired, beleaguered, and hungry, were nonetheless forced to act, to make choices, to listen to what was necessary and true. These stories give concrete examples of human beings who, mindful and awake, could make good, clear choices in spite of weariness and thirst. We are invited to imagine that we, too, can do things well, and that our life will then emerge in a particular way. And if we do things badly or without paying close attention, we will find our lives straying in unwanted directions. These are the elemental physics of spiritual practice. The practice of dealing with temptation gives us an opportunity to uncover the work of these essential principles in our own lives.

Spiritual practice is a careful study of how things work at the most essential level. If we study the lives of most spiritual teachers, we will discover they had little interest in starting new religions. Rather, they were attempting to discern, with precision and accuracy, how each simple act we perform every day has enormous impact on how our lives evolve, how everything we do shapes the world around us.

TEMPTATIONS AS TEACHERS

Why do certain things tempt one person and not another? Some of us are tempted by fame, while others seem content with anonymity. Some of us are tempted by power, while others are happy to avoid responsibility altogether. Some are seduced by the pursuit of riches, while others prefer a simpler life.

Temptations can be our greatest teachers. We can discover a great deal about ourselves if we carefully observe which temptations are, for us, the most appealing. Which desires are most seductive? Most difficult to resist? Which people, things, or experiences literally capture our attention, dissolve our will, and corrode any vow or promise we have made to ourselves or others?

Temptations reveal where we are caught, stuck, or troubled by some unfinished inner business. Something in us needs to be healed or completed. Those things that tempt are clear mirrors that can serve us well. They reflect back to us those gaps in our serenity where we are still grasping on the outside for what has not yet been made fully whole on the inside.

The mirrors of temptation show us something about ourselves. If we are married and find ourselves attracted to another, the fact that we are drawn to have an affair reveals something about how we feel about our relationship. If we are successful at work and yet crave more and more power, it may indicate that we are afflicted with fear, insecurity, or greed. If we are easily enticed by food to the point of overeating, we may discover some potent emptiness within us that aches to be filled.

The irony is that people who are driven to make money are rarely satisfied no matter how much they acquire. They still labor within a prison of scarcity and strive to keep increasing their riches to the point of absurdity. Similarly, those who crave food or sex are rarely satiated, and it is not long after eating or lovemaking that their bottomless hunger reasserts itself. Desire is rarely satisfied by the object of desire; desire is gratified only when we cultivate an inner sense of serenity and contentment with whatever we have.

Temptation, then, is not God's way of leading us into failure and punishment. The things that tempt us can be our teachers and our guides, challenging us to discern how things work in our heart, mind, and soul. Temptation serves as a spiritual CAT scan, revealing those things hidden beneath our conscious awareness that remain unfinished or unacknowledged.

The cost, then, of succumbing to temptation is not that we end up as sinners. The cost is that we end up chasing useless things. We grasp on the outside for what may only be made whole from the inside. This is why we struggle in prayer to listen for the right thing, the true understanding, the honest response. We can spend our time creating beauty, healing, planting, loving, dancing, and growing—or we can waste time striving after wind.

If we do not become still, if we do not pray or meditate, if we are lazy and easily seduced by temptation, we will construct a shaky identity forged with fame, desperation, sexual conquest, material goods, accomplishments, and ambitions.

TEMPTED BY THE LIGHT

So how do we hear the phrase *Lead us not into temptation*? Perhaps we might pray instead *Do not let us fall into temptation*. Here, we are praying for strength and clarity, for the reliable companionship of the Divine within us, for courage to face those moments in which we make fundamental choices—choices about who we are, what we love, and how we shall live.

The riches of the world are seductive and compelling. When we are tempted by what would fill us temporarily and then leave us empty, we pray to remember who we are, and listen for the wisdom to choose correctly. When we wrestle successfully with temptation, we discover clarity, strength, and wisdom.

In the Christian tradition, one image of the Tempter is Lucifer. Lucifer was the angel closest to God, cast out of heaven because of his vanity and pride. Lucifer literally means "light-bearing," the one who *looks* like the light, but merely reflects the light of the Divine. After his fall from grace, Lucifer became infinitely dangerous, because while Lucifer appears to bear the light, he has, in fact, no light at all.

Most of us are more reliably drawn off-center by those things that appear, at first blush, to be good things. Look at the temptations of Jesus—to turn stones to bread, perhaps to feed the poor and hungry; to have the angels reveal how valuable he was, maybe to help him gain positive, healing influence with the religious authorities; or to have the power to govern the kingdoms of the earth, which he would surely do with more wisdom, justice, and mercy than all the corrupt monarchs of his day.

The temptations of Jesus are tempting precisely because they look good. The attractions most difficult for us to resist are not the glaringly obvious and destructive acts of murder, hatred, or robbery. More alluring are the "little white lies," the subtle, daily seductions that are most likely to pull us off balance. The impulse to take credit for something someone else has done, to shade the truth to make ourselves look better than we are, to deftly step over someone else to gain a larger measure of influence, or to create an illusion of spiritual achievement that transcends who we really are. These and a thousand others like them are our most challenging temptations: Trade just a little bit of what you truly hold sacred, and you can have it all.

Whenever we are presented with anything that will further our ambitions, our career, our popularity, power, or influence, we are called to pause before we act. Spiritual practice is, in part, a laboratory. If we make a choice that proves right for ourselves and for others, it will rarely appear again. But if we choose foolishly, the same choice will often present itself again and again until we learn the lesson of choosing well.

So we are invited, through endless decisions, to live well every day, to note our shortcomings, make amends, repair what feels broken, make things right. Each day, through the crucible of temptation, we are invited to live in a new way, to make new choices. Finally, perhaps we pray this prayer as a simple plea for strength and clarity: This is our prayer: *Do not let us fall into temptation. When called away from right action, right speech, right livelihood, grant us the wisdom to be still, to find courage and clarity, to remember we are already beloved children of a loving Creator, fed by our daily bread, welcome in the household of heaven.*

Prayer Practice

When in prayer, allow the mind to wander until it settles on an object of temptation. It may be a habit, a desire, a craving that has proven painful or depleting, yet remains a gnawing thirst in your body or heart. Choose something that is particularly alluring and difficult to resist.

Follow your breath, centering your awareness in the present moment. Rest in the rhythm of the visceral sensation of the inhale and exhale. As you settle into mindfulness of the present moment, allow the object of temptation to appear before you. Notice what shifts or changes in your mind or body. Be aware of how and where desire arises within you. Watch how whatever tempts you evokes a response—a sadness, an ache, an emptiness, a yearning. Take a moment to explore where that yearning lives in the body, in the mind, in the heart.

When you feel the tug of desire, bring your awareness back to your breathing, or back to a word or phrase in centering prayer. When we pray, we return again and again to the present moment. Here, now, we are in heaven. There is nothing wanting. Desire and temptation are *always* grounded in some future gratification. Desire beckons us to leap into the future; prayer liberates us to return to the blessing of the present moment.

DELIVER US FROM EVIL

When we honestly and courageously
face the evils we have nourished
in ourselves and in the world,
we begin to plant the seeds of
heaven on earth.

What exactly is evil? The very word makes many of us squeamish. In our hyperpsychologized culture, we shy away from using the term at all, preferring to look to ignorance, illness, or emotional pathology to explain the ways we inflict unspeakable pain on one another. We feel more comfortable imagining that humans cannot really be evil, only confused, stupid, or sick.

Ignorance, illness, and pathology are things we can control, things we can cure or repair. If we just apply education, medicine, or some other social policy, we can make these things better, mitigate the harm they can do, make them go away.

But if there is such a thing as evil—some powerfully

destructive force loose in the world that eludes our clever treatments and interventions—then we are suddenly powerless before something terrifying and dangerous. If we stand face to face with genuine evil, we are thrust into a world where our lives, and our families, and our civilization are no longer safe. We can never feel completely secure. If evil exists, there are no guarantees. There is no place to hide.

The existence of evil not only places us in danger of being destroyed by evil forces; it also means that we ourselves are capable of evil. The implications of our own complicity in evil are so horrifying that we mitigate the horror by using emasculating psychological language.

At the same time, our reluctance to use the word *evil* is understandable. History is riddled with examples of peoples, nations, and communities far too quick to judge any person or group with different skin, different religious beliefs, or a different nationality as "evil." Erik Erikson called this tendency "pseudospeciation," the corrosive capacity of the mind to assert that one group of people is somehow less human, not as fully evolved as ourselves—to make them "pseudohuman," if you will.

When we label others in this way, we grant ourselves a terrible internal permission and justification to exploit, enslave, oppress, or even exterminate the "other." The world is saturated with stories of people who, claiming God on their side, demonized their enemies by calling them pollutants, cancers infecting a godly and peaceful world. Then they purged, cleansed, and purified the earth through the enslavement and genocide of the less-than-human, "evil" enemies that stood in their way. So it is morally imperative that we understand how we use the term *evil,* for it has enabled us to do so much damage, to so many, for so long.

EVIL IN THE WORLD

In our own age, we have crafted new ways to pursue the evils of war by using children as weapons. All over the world children are kidnapped, abducted, and trained to be soldiers for causes they cannot understand. They are forced to fight, to kill, to make war on behalf of those who shield themselves from its dangers even as they demand its spoils. A friend who works in East Timor gave me a gift of a beautifully delicate shawl, green and yellow and blue, woven by hand by a group of rural village women. She tells me that soldiers roam the country, regularly coming to this village and so many others, to recruit children, demanding of the village parents: "Give us twenty boys to fight, twenty girls to provide us sex, or we will destroy your village, we will kill you all."

Until World War II, most of the casualties of war were combatants, killed in war zones. Today, a shocking majority of the victims of war are children and women, noncombatants. This is the despicable cowardice of war, the cowardice of evil.

But evil is not confined to wars between peoples and nations. Evil can arise in subtle, more intimately corrosive forms. When my friend Eugene first went to Westminster Seminary, his family was justly proud that he was the first in his poor African-American family to go to such a college. When the time came for Eugene to leave home, they gave him a hero's blessing, and sent him with a trunk filled with books and supplies for his new life.

When Eugene got to his room and settled in, he opened the trunk his family had packed for him. There, among the clothes and books, were twenty-one jars of Pond's vanishing cream. Westminster Seminary was a white institution, and Eugene was the only black student. His family, wanting desperately for him to fit in, hoped that a regular application of the vanishing cream would make his skin lighter and lighter—perhaps even light enough so he could pass as white, pass as someone worthy, someone not like them.

This is the result of the evil that can live in our culture, giving birth to a thousand tiny evils that infect our daily lives. It makes it impossible to accuse any one person of evil, because we hide behind a society afflicted with injustice that acts as our surrogate, and enfolds us all in an insidious complicity in institutional harm done quietly, invisibly, ceaselessly.

Deliver us from evil. Here, we are yearning to be delivered from the corrosive fears that would destroy our peace, our families, our lives. We also ask to be delivered from those who would threaten us without thought, without regret. *Deliver us from those who would attack us on the street, from those who would kidnap our children, who would invade our homes, rob us of our possessions, our safety, our peace, our hope.*

EVIL IN OURSELVES

But what about our need to be delivered from the evil in ourselves, in our own hearts, our own communities? We are reluctant to imagine we are capable of evil; we cannot bear to confess that we can inflict harm upon others in the same way our enemies have done to us.

If we are rigorous and honest with ourselves, through clear and courageous reflection, we may very well find we are capable of closing and hardening our own hearts in ways that bring injury, intentionally or unintentionally, to others, even to those we love dearly. Every one of us can be cruel and impatient, angry and destructive in our words, thoughts, and actions. We can, in times of inner torment, be filled with hatred, intolerance, and destructive impulses that can bleed into our relationships with the world. Who among us has not committed some cruel, destructive act for which we later feel ashamed, recognizing with deep sadness and regret that we, too, have destroyed or broken something precious, or have brought terrible harm to another?

How do we pray for healing, for some cleansing of this evil in ourselves? Many spiritual traditions suggest that evil springs most swiftly from a heart that has been hardened. When Moses pleaded with Pharaoh to free the Hebrew slaves from bondage, Pharaoh's heart was hardened; as a result, great suffering was visited upon the slaves, and later, upon Pharaoh and his people. Similarly, Jesus told his disciples that many Pharisees would, because of the hardness of their hearts, turn against him. This hardness of heart enabled certain religious and Roman authorities to conspire to arrest, torture, and kill Jesus for his teachings.

A hardened heart denies the suffering it causes. It will not apprehend the consequences of what it has done. This refusal to acknowledge the fruits of our actions becomes the seed of evil. Therefore, when we pray *Deliver us from evil,* we must honestly and courageously name the evils we have chosen to nourish in our own lives and our own communities. Only then can we honorably claim to plant seeds of heaven in the soil of the earth.

GOD AND EVIL

Elie Wiesel tells a story about a group of Jews in a concentration camp who, after years of suffering torture, humiliation, and death, decided to put God on trial. They created a mock courtroom, called witnesses, and heard testimony of God's indifference, his absence, even his complicity in this unspeakable evil. In the end, with much anguish and weeping, they pronounced God guilty; a criminal in the eyes of all humanity.

And then, in the silence that followed, they prayed.

We are humbled by the presence of an ultimate paradox. If there is genuine evil at work in the world, how can there be a loving God watching over us all? But if we cease to rely on God, to whom, then, can we pray? Living with evil is excruciating, yet living even a single day without the spiritual companionship and support of a loving God is unthinkable.

If we allow ourselves to succumb to the bitter legacy of evil, we live as if we were already dead, without a light in our eye, without hope in our hearts. Kathleen Kostelny, a dear friend and colleague, shared a story she wrote that arose out of her work with children of war in Guatemala. She describes the life of Flor, a young girl in a village devastated by the violence of years of government conflict. The story begins as Flor finds her parents murdered by soldiers:

When the sun moved down the mountain, she ran to the fields to greet her parents—her mother would scold her for running so fast, and her father would scoop her up in his strong arms. Her mother and father lay on the soft brown earth. *"Levante! Levante!"* Get up! Get up! she demanded. They did not move, even when she began to cry.

When her brother came back from market, he held her to his chest and rocked her all night, murmuring, *"Pobrecita, pobrecita"*—poor little one—until the sun came up.

They buried their parents the next day in the fields of corn under the bilboa tree. That night her brother told her that he was going away to be a soldier.

It had been three years since the soldiers came to her finca in the mountains, and since her brother went away. The sun danced on Flor's fingers as she gently cradled a butterfly of vivid blues and purples in her tiny brown hands.

"Pobrecita," poor little one, she laughed, taking the creature between her small fingers, then pausing briefly before ripping the trembling wing from its body and letting it drop to the soft earth.

The butterfly struggled to free itself with its remaining wing, even as the little fingers peeled it slowly from its body. She dropped the lifeless remains, then, with her bare foot, crushed the useless body in the soft Guatemalan dirt.

Like the Jews in the concentration camp, we must refuse to surrender to evil, the prison of ultimate despair. This is our prayer: *Deliver us from the temptation to feel crushed under the weight of what we have been given. Deliver us from the complete disbelief in anything good, whole, or sacred. Deliver us from that time when, at the end of the day, we can no longer pray.*

Prayer Practice

Thomas Merton wrote, "Pure love and prayer are learned in the hour when prayer becomes impossible and the heart has turned to stone."

Dr. Elkhanan Elkes was the revered elder of the Kovno Ghetto in Lithuania. He served as a physician and spiritual leader to countless prisoners in the camps. He faced his captors always with dignity and courage, tirelessly serving those in need. The story of his life and work is honored in the Holocaust Museum in Washington, D.C.

Dr. Joel Elkes, his son, wrote of his family's life before, during, and after the camps. Here, he writes about his mother, as she tells him what nourished her spirit in the face of captivity and the loss of her beloved husband:

> She told me that, apart from the hope of seeing her husband and us, two objects sustained her in captivity. One was a piece of bread, which she always hid about her person; the other a broken piece of comb. She kept the bread in case someone needed it more than she; and, no matter what, morning and night, she would comb her hair to affirm her person.

We cannot go empty-handed into the country of evil. We must carry what we can, small things that sustain and nourish us, that can affirm what is beautiful and necessary, good and true. What small thing do you carry that you can give yourself and others? Each of us has some gift to lift up the dignity and worth of those who have been scarred by evil.

We can ground our prayer, *Deliver us from evil,* in a single gesture of kindness, courage, or faith. With this crust of bread and broken comb we deny that evil can starve or dishonor us. With a word of kindness or the lighting of a candle, we can dissolve the corrosive effects of darkness and evil. Evil can prosper only when hearts are willing to remain hard and unresponsive. Every act of kindness, courageously offered, however small, is a small flower sown in a field of peace. In the face of evil, our life becomes our prayer.

FOR THINE IS THE KINGDOM, THE POWER, AND THE GLORY

Everything—love, joy, sorrow, grace, the earth, life itself—all belongs to God.

When I was a small boy, as I recited the Lord's Prayer in church, it seemed that at this point we were turning the corner and heading for home. I didn't pay as much attention to the *For thine is the kingdom* part as I did to the beginning of the prayer. Maybe a boy's attention span had stretched to its spiritual limit, or perhaps I was finished with praying and ready to move on to the next hymn. I loved singing hymns more than praying, so I was ready to wrap it up and get to the music.

But perhaps, even as a boy, I sensed the deeper shift here, where we do, in fact, round the corner and head for home. Prayer is a living thing which, like all living things, moves in rhythm with life—the beat of the heart, the cadence of the inhale and exhale, the seasons, the tides, the sun and moon all sway in life-giving rhythm. When we center down into our deep, still places to pray, even our prayers fall into synchronous rhythm with the heartbeat of creation.

The Lord's Prayer has a rhythm. It begins with a yearning to enter into quiet communion with our Creator, the loving parent, the spirit of healing, the God who lives in the grace of all things, who knows our every move and watches over us with love:

> *Our Father,*
> *who art in heaven,*
> *Hallowed be thy name.*
> *Thy kingdom come,*
> *thy will be done,*
> *on earth, as it is in heaven.*

The beginning of our prayer is about God; we offer our respect and reverence for all those qualities of the divine spirit, enormously potent and protective, that sustain us, the world, and the universe.

The second part of the prayer is about us. We bring our needs and concerns to the altar of our relationship with God. We lift up our heart's desire for ourselves and those we love, we lift up our fear and grief, our joy and thanksgiving. Here, we bring ourselves before the feet of the teacher, and ask for what we need to live life fully and well:

> *Give us this day our daily bread.*
> *And forgive us our trespasses,*
> *as we forgive those who trespass against us.*
> *And lead us not into temptation,*
> *but deliver us from evil.*

Finally, as we close the circle of prayer, we turn our attention once again to God. The rhythm of prayer, the rhythm of all life, moves in this way. Having spilled out the contents of our own heart, we place our trust once again in the care of God. However life evolves, whatever answer we receive, we confess that it all belongs to God, and not to us. We humbly release our will to the loving Spirit that nourishes us and consecrates every moment of our lives. In the end, it is all up to the Creator:

> *For thine is the kingdom,*
> *the power, and the glory,*
> *forever and ever.*
> *Amen.*

FOR THINE IS THE KINGDOM

Throughout these pages, we have reimagined the "kingdom of God" as the "household of heaven," a place where every child of creation is welcomed home for sanctuary, nourishment, and care. So when we pray *For thine is the kingdom,* we are truly saying *Thank you for welcoming us, with love, into your household.*

Many of us spend our lives desperately seeking peace, looking everywhere for signs of God's presence, striving to find the words, rituals, or practices that will unlock the secret of divine grace and finally reveal the hidden treasure of God's loving company.

But this desperate search for God implies that God is *not already fully present,* right here in our lives this instant. In truth, our Creator is always a part of us, right here, right now, as close as our heart, as close as our breath.

As members of God's household we have been given everything: life, love, food, clothing, beauty, grace, forgiveness—and, yes, also suffering, fear, illness, and loss. Here, we are invited to gather around the table, take our place in the household of heaven, and give thanks for God's companionship through all our gifts and the challenges. We recall the words of Soto, a beloved Buddhist nun, whose singular prayer was simply this: *Thank you for everything. I have no complaint whatsoever.*

This is how we enter the household of God. We bring our hearts, honest and open, and await our welcome in the place of our deepest belonging, beloved for who we are, awake and prepared to receive nourishment and healing.

Here, at the close of prayer, we allow ourselves to rest in this single, astonishing truth: We are living in God's household, we are beloved children in that household, and we will not be left comfortless.

FOR THINE IS THE POWER AND THE GLORY

Ours is also a prayer of humility. We are human, humble, from the Latin *humus,* meaning "earth" or "soil." To be humble is to feel ourselves part of creation, a member of a large family of creatures who live in, on, and above the earth, neither inferior nor superior. We are simply one of the family.

We live in a world not entirely of our own making. We are every day transported into territory we could not possibly have planned or imagined. We are reminded of this daily in little ways, when we are surprised by joy, or when our plans go awry, or our work is interrupted. We are reminded in larger ways, as when my friend Maria, a member of a breast cancer support group, says that she sometimes catches herself looking around the room, wondering, *Who among us will die first?*

All healing, all grace, all glory comes from God. Our work is not to create the world, but to live well in it. We are not the head of this family. We are more likely to find heaven on earth when we begin to trust in forces larger than ourselves, forces wise and good, that shape the currency of our days. When we pray, we consent to be taken. We consent to be surprised. We place our lives in the hands of a loving God.

Jesus said, *The wind blows where it will, and you hear the sound of it, but do not know whence it comes, or whither it goes. So it is with the life of the Spirit.* There are forces before which we bend with faith and humility, forces beyond our comprehension or control. When we pray, we feel how the turning of the world, the turning of our lives, is tenderly crafted perfectly for us.

And so, in the end, just a few simple teachings

provide us with all we will ever need. Love God, and love your neighbor as yourself. Offer your gifts to the family of the earth. Forgive those who hurt you. Seek first the household of God, and all the treasures of the universe shall be given you. You are welcome, this is your home, and all will be well.

Prayer Practice

People who are recovering from addiction often seek healing for themselves through prayer, community support, and the sharing of stories of sorrow and hope. When there inevitably comes a moment when they must confront problems or difficulties too enormous or complex to be solved, they invoke a phrase: *Turn it over.*

If it is too big to fix or too heavy to bear, they say, turn it over to God. We all carry the weight of extraordinary sorrows and losses, challenges unmet, responsibilities unfulfilled. If we work every problem as if the solution is up to us, we will quickly become weary and depleted, exhausted and overwhelmed.

The kingdom, power, and glory all belong to God. When God wants a thing done, when the time is full and the season of birth and renewal has come, the speed with which things happen can take our breath away. In prayer, we humbly offer what we cannot do ourselves, and place our burdens in hands larger and wiser than our own.

FOREVER AND EVER, AMEN

*We are, always and forever,
through the practice of prayer, invited
to rest in the loving arms of our Creator.*

Here, at the end of prayer, we dissolve, like salt in a clear mountain lake, into the comforting spaciousness of eternity.

At the end of our lives we will count as priceless only those things grown in the fertile soil of time. We will remember shared love, nurtured only in time. We will recall our deep friendships, leavened with time. We will reap the harvest of our honesty, tenderness, intimacy, generosity, wisdom, all blessings of a human life ripened in the astonishingly gratuitous seasons of time.

When we pray to a Creator who lives forever and ever, we honor a love that will guide us for all eternity. We are invoking not only a quantity, but also a quality, of time. In prayer, we shape the way time moves. When our prayers are lived on earth, as in heaven, prayer can take birth in time spent on a walk on the beach, an afternoon with a loved one, a languid summer evening, or a cup of tea by a winter's fire.

For Buddhists, the arc of time is immense, measured in *kalpas,* enormous spans of years that the Buddha described in this way: "Imagine a mountain a mile high, a mile wide, and a mile deep. Now, imagine that a bird, with a piece of fine silk in its beak, flies beside the mountain, allowing the silk to gently brush against it. This happens once every hundred years. The time it would take for that bird, and that silk, to wear this enormous mountain completely to the ground—this is one *kalpa.*"

The teaching, of course, is that we live and pray in a field of eternity where urgency and desperation seem like folly. The seasons of spiritual growth and healing go on forever, through days, years, lifetimes.

Jesus offered a similar teaching to his disciples. Shortly before he was killed, he was sharing a meal with them at the home of Simon, a leper. A woman, presumably Mary Magdalene, arrived bearing an alabaster flask containing expensive ointment. She broke open the exquisite flask and anointed Jesus' head with the precious oil. His disciples became angry with him, saying: *Why this waste? This ointment may have been sold for a large sum, and the money given to the poor.* But Jesus responded, *Why do you trouble this woman? She has done a beautiful thing for me. You will always have the poor with you, but you will not always have me.*

When Jesus proclaims, *The poor will always be with you,* he is not saying we should forget the poor and only worry about ourselves. The core of Jesus' life and death was offered in service to the poor, the hungry, and the dispossessed. Instead, he is reminding us that *our work is never done.* As long as there is life, there will be children to raise, hungry people to feed, the lonely to be comforted, and the sick to be healed. The work of healing and service is an essential part of our incarnation; it is simply what we do. While this endlessness may at first seem distressing—we are condemned to never get all our work done—the eternal nature of service actually liberates us. It gives us permission to rest, to leave our good and necessary work behind. Just as there is a time for every purpose under heaven, there is always time to pray, to rest, to be nourished and refreshed. Whenever we return, the work will be there, waiting.

Throughout our lives things arise in their season, require a particular kind of care, and then move on. Thus, *forever and ever* is a challenge to the ways we constrict and hoard time. When we live in *forever and ever,* we lose the corrosive rush and hurry that contaminate our days. *Forever and ever* allows us to live our life and offer our gifts easily and without hurry. When we place our gifts, however small, beside countless gifts offered before and after, they will germinate and blossom for millennia, in ways we could never imagine.

AMEN

We are all accustomed to hearing the word *Amen* at the close of prayer. It seems tacked on almost as an afterthought, a sign the prayer is over, time to raise your head and open your eyes.

But the *Amen* was not traditionally spoken by the priest or rabbi; rather, it was a response spoken by the people in affirmation of the prayer that had been offered. It was an assent, an agreement among those present that what had been spoken was honorable and true.

When we say *Amen,* we declare the power and sacred intention of the prayer in our hearts. We acknowledge everything—our dependence upon a loving God, our yearning to feel welcome in the household of heaven, our need for daily bread, our willingness to forgive, our thirst for courage and wisdom and safety, and our willingness to be led wherever we need to go.

When we say *Amen,* we are saying *Mother-Father God, we have spoken the truth of our deepest heart. We have come for food and guidance, and we have submitted our heart's desire to your loving will for our lives. Use us as instruments of your peace. We pray for ourselves and for the healing of the world. Merciful Spirit, loving Creator, beloved God, we are yours, now and always.*

Hear our prayer.

And then let us say, with our words, with our hearts, indeed, with our very lives:

Amen.

ACKNOWLEDGMENTS

As always, whenever I endeavor to write anything I hope will be honorable and true, I find myself indebted to countless friends and companions. When I tried to list each and every person who taught me to pray, who shared their stories with me, and who nourished and sustained me during the writing of this book, I gathered a list of names that ran to four pages. So let me simply say this: You know who you are, and I love you all.

And so a few simple thanks are left to be spoken. First, to Lakshmi for her patience and companionship as an editor.

Second, I could not have written this book without Marianna Cacciatore. Indeed, I could do very little at all without her. She not only runs Bread for the Journey with boundless wisdom and enthusiasm, she is a jewel who helps guide my life, manages my career, counsels and supports everyone, and laughs at my jokes. One could not dream of a more bountiful selection of gifts bound up in one single person.

I am indebted to my children, Sherah and Maxwell, for their endless patience with all the time I spend at my desk. I love them both with all my heart, and pray for their continued willingness to put up with having a writer as their father.

I am eternally grateful, as always, to Toni Burbank for her clear eye and her undying faith in me and my writing. I am lucky and honored to have her as my editor, critic, and good friend.

And finally, words cannot express the love and devotion I feel for my dear friend and agent Loretta Barrett, without whom this book would literally never have been written. She saw something no one else could see, and I am the better for it. If you find anything at all of value in these words, thanks go to Loretta.

ABOUT THE AUTHOR

WAYNE MULLER is an ordained minister and a therapist, a graduate of Harvard Divinity School, and the founder of Bread for the Journey, a nationwide organization serving people and communities in need. He has also served as Spiritual Care Consultant at the Betty Ford Center, Senior Scholar at the Fetzer Institute, and Fellow of the Institute of Noetic Sciences. He runs the Institute for Engaged Spirituality and gives lectures and retreats nationwide. He is the author of *Legacy of the Heart,* a *New York Times* bestseller; *How, Then, Shall We Live?;* and *Sabbath.*

BREAD FOR THE JOURNEY supports community-based, neighborhood philanthropy by encouraging the natural generosity of ordinary people. There are now twenty chapters of Bread for the Journey in the United States and Canada. For locations, and for information about starting a Bread for the Journey chapter in your community, please write or call:

Bread for the Journey
267 Miller Avenue
Mill Valley, CA 94941
Phone: 415-383-4600
HYPERLINK:
http://www.breadforthejourney.org

You can also contact Bread for the Journey for a list of Wayne Muller's retreats, workshops, books, and tapes.